PENGUIN BOOKS

C'EST LA VIE

Suzy Gershman is an American author, journalist and television personality who has brought her international expertise to readers, television viewers, travelers, and shoppers the world over with her series of Frommer's Born to Shop books. She has appeared on *Oprah*, CNN, the *Today* show, CBS *Morning News*, and *Good Morning America* and has been featured in *People, USA Today, Family Circle, McCall's,* and the *International Herald Tribune*. She also writes travel pieces for *Where Paris* and *Air France Madame*, both English language magazines published in France. In 2001 she bought a house in Provence, where she spends the summer cooking, writing, doing crafts projects, and going to flea markets. Gershman lives with her dog, Samantha Joe Cocker Spaniel, who loves to eat, sleep, and shop—just like Suzy.

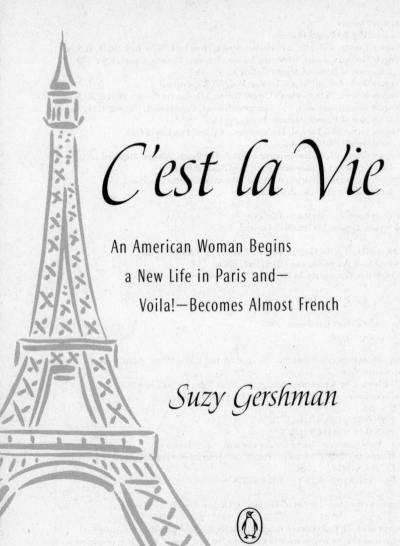

C'est la Vie

An American Woman Begins
a New Life in Paris and—
Voila!—Becomes Almost French

Suzy Gershman

Penguin Books

PENGUIN BOOKS
Published by the Penguin Group
Penguin Group (USA) Inc., 375 Hudson Street, New York, New York 10014, U.S.A.
Penguin Group (Canada), 10 Alcorn Avenue, Toronto, Ontario, Canada M4V 3B2
    (a division of Pearson Penguin Canada Inc.)
Penguin Books Ltd, 80 Strand, London WC2R 0RL, England
Penguin Ireland, 25 St Stephen's Green, Dublin 2, Ireland (a division of Penguin Books Ltd)
Penguin Group (Australia), 250 Camberwell Road, Camberwell, Victoria 3124, Australia
    (a division of Pearson Australia Group Pty Ltd)
Penguin Books India Pvt Ltd, 11 Community Centre, Panchsheel Park,
    New Delhi - 110 017, India
Penguin Group (N.Z.) cnr Airborne and Rosedale Roads, Albany, Auckland 1310,
    New Zealand (a division of Pearson New Zealand Ltd)
Penguin Books (South Africa) (Pty) Ltd, 24 Sturdee Avenue, Rosebank,
    Johannesburg 2196, South Africa

Penguin Books Ltd, Registered Offices:
80 Strand, London WC2R 0RL, England

First published in the United States of America by Viking Penguin,
a member of Penguin Group (USA) Inc., 2004
Published in Penguin Books 2005

10 9 8 7 6 5 4 3 2

Copyright © Suzy Gershman, 2004
All rights reserved

THE LIBRARY OF CONGRESS HAS CATALOGED THE HARDCOVER EDITION AS FOLLOWS:
Gershman, Suzy.
C'est la vie : An American conquers the city of light, begins a new life,
and becomes—*zut alors!*—almost French / Suzy Gershman.
    p.   cm.
    ISBN 0-670-03269-7 (hc.)
    ISBN 0 14 30.3550 9 (pbk.)
    1. Paris (France)—Social life and customs—20th century.   2. Gershman, Suzy—
    Homes and haunts—France—Paris.   3. Americans—France—Paris.   I. Title.
    DC718.A44G47   2004
    944'.361083'9—dc21   2003053774

Printed in the United States of America • Designed by Nancy Resnick

For Claire, who got me through it

Merci, remerci et gros bisous

Contents

C'est la Vie

To Start With

I did not have to reinvent myself to move to Paris. In fact, it was far easier than I imagined. I spoke some version of French—Official Bad French—and the rest just sort of, well, just sort of flowed . . . like the Seine to the sea.

I always knew that one day I would live in France. This was not a dream on my part, but a fact of life, not whispered in the winds of chance, but firmly written on the mistral of my life. I used to tear up when I heard Judy Collins sing plaintively the refrain that went, "My father always promised us that we would live in France . . ." When I heard Billy Joel sing, "Vienna waits for you," I knew what he meant.

I knew that Paris was my Vienna, it was waiting for me.

I had been coming to France several times a year for more than thirty years. As each year passed by, France became more and more a part of my life—my business life, as well as my social life. I would get weepy when I left; I felt that I *needed* to come back. I had a good life, but it tasted even better in France.

I was never a Francophile or Franco-freak, one of those people who dream of all things French or think a product is better because it's French. But through my work on the Born to Shop series of travel guides, a lot of Frenchmen (and women) came into my life. Some became friends. Despite differences in language, religion and background, I felt a connection with them that I didn't share with most Americans.

I was also seduced by a lifestyle that seemed a lot more sophisticated than the long-range future I pictured for myself in the United States—bingo on Wednesdays, the early bird special at five P.M. and the last years of my life spent in a retirement community, alone, waiting for the chocolate pudding to be served. I knew I would never be rich, so the French ideal of a small piece of life with good food, good friends and real butter seemed more and more attractive.

About ten years ago, I became seriously interested in the idea of retirement in France. I grimly suspected that my husband— some ten years older than I—would predecease me. That would leave me a relatively young woman, alone and in need of a plan. Not that you can ever fully prepare yourself for the death of your beloved, but having the skeleton of a notion of what to do next was comforting.

I knew I could never live in Florida. I have naturally curly hair. Besides, France is a smarter place to spend your golden years: it has socialized medicine and the prunes are soaked in cognac.

I learned somewhat to speak French when I was fifty, a diffi-cult task for anyone over the age of six; a chore my friend Marie called "an excellent right-brain activity for a middle-aged woman." I didn't do it as a mental exercise. I did it to take a step forward. I've never been good with languages or music. I was a disaster with rhythm sticks as a child; I was no better with the difference between *être* and *aller*. To compensate, I memorized lyrics to Johnny Hallyday songs and tried to analyze the words to the childhood song Frère Jacques. I am still not sure if those bells were ringing in the morning (*matin*) or ringing out the matins church service, but never mind.

Then I began a self-education process beyond language and culture. I learned the metric system. I became a whiz at turning kilometers into miles in a nanosecond. I got my colleague Patricia Wells, the American Queen of French Cuisine, to promise she would teach me to make a *tarte tatin*. I got ready emotionally to give up my big, heavy Volvo wagon to someday drive a small, sneaky Peugeot, the kind that could make it through narrow medieval *allées* and into tightly fashioned French parking spaces.

My husband, Mike, traveled with me to France frequently, but we did not share the same long-range retirement dreams. When I took him to a friend's home in the hills near St. Paul de Vence on the Riviera and said, "I want to live just like this someday," he shrugged, turned away and said, "I don't."

But he didn't want to live in Florida either . . . and I knew I could change his mind someday. Surely he was joking when he suggested Cooperstown, New York—home of the Baseball Hall of Fame—as an alternative. France would prevail, I was certain. In our marriage, I was the one with the "brilliant" ideas and he was the one with the brakes. But he always came around. So I began a silent fantasy life; you might call me the Walter Mitty of the Midi. I thought up ways to get to France and ways to convince Mike that he too had to come try it. What lifestyle would work for both of us?

Would it be a whitewashed apartment in Nice, in the Cimiez district overlooking the sea, with perhaps a water view? Or maybe a stone house, at least three hundred years old, in Provence . . . in a tiny town, with curvy streets and pastel-painted buildings with contrasting shutters? Petunias or pansies? Perhaps I should settle for Paris and grand Haussmannian style: chimneys in every room, high, high ceilings, a balcony dancing with geraniums and rooms heavy with moldings and rosettes—those plaster curlicues we normally saw only in museums or decorating magazines?

But then, if my husband, Mike, didn't really want to go to France, maybe I would be an old lady by the time I retired or was widowed. Maybe I would end up in Cannes, at the Hesperides Maison de Retraite—the retirement home handily located on the city's second-best shopping street, where you can cook in your kitchenette or go to the dining room or have meals served to you in bed. You could walk half a block down the street to a branch of the famed pâtisserie LeNotre for cafeteria service. Needless to say, I didn't want to wait that long. And I really wanted Mike to be with me; all the best times of my life were spent with him. Besides, his French was better than mine.

Eventually, I convinced my husband that we should try one year together in Paris—if only so that I could get it out of my system. I hit him with this at just the right time—his forced retirement was coming up, he had a no-compete clause in his contract, and he didn't know what to do with himself or what path to follow next. Living in Paris for a year while he thought it over suddenly seemed like a *bonne idée.* "Vienna waits for you," I whispered.

We giggled with anticipation when we talked about the apartment we would take in Paris—something small, something cheap. We would return to BoHo days in middle age, living on wine and cheese and love . . . and a small allowance we were setting aside. We talked a lot about the details. Where would live? Left Bank or Right? Were we too old to walk up stairs? How many flights could we handle? Did we need a room for guests? For our son? Would I cook or would we eat market meals and picnics most days with a few odd nights out to visit some chef friends?

I was sure we'd have so much fun that Mike would agree to all my retirement schemes well before our year was up. We were young—okay, we were middle-aged, but we thought we were young—and healthy and still crazy about each other after all these twenty-five years. I thought we would grow old together, spend the years watching our son become a famous musician-songwriter and travel back and forth between the United States and France, with train trips to all the European cities we loved or had missed. Maybe I would open a store. Mike wanted to write guidebooks for the flood of baby boomers he was certain would come to Europe. The Young Farts Guides he called them. We thought we had the best years of our lives ahead of us.

We were wrong.

Suddenly, Mike was stricken with nonsymptomatic lung cancer; he was in stage four (terminal) before the cancer was ever diagnosed. He died three months after discovery of the mass in his chest and only six weeks after the official diagnosis. Each night of those three months I lay in his arms and sobbed.

"What will I do without you?" I wailed.

"You will go to Paris," he said tenderly, night after night, while brushing the tears from my face and pushing back my hair urgently—as if he wanted to help me solve one more problem. "Paris waits for you."

Mike died at 5:55 A.M. on the morning of January 4, 2000. He died at home, peacefully and in his sleep. He simply stopped snoring. The sound of his silence woke me up. I held him in my arms while our orange cat, Pyewacket, sat on his lap. We all cuddled together for about an hour, me with my head on Mike's chest, trying to hear a heartbeat, knowing I would never be rescued by his strength again. When his feet got cold, I knew for sure.

I took his wedding ring from his left hand, removed my wedding ring from my left hand and switched both of them over to my right hand to signify our marriage had crossed over to the spiritual realm. His larger band was held in place by my smaller one. At 7:30 A.M. I called his doctor.

"He's dead?" the doctor asked, stunned.

"I don't think he's faking," I managed to say.

Never die the first week in January. You have to earn out the health insurance deductible all over again. You have to pay taxes for the entire year. It really ruins the holidays for your family.

Okay, okay, so I paid for the funeral with a credit card, it's true. I wanted the miles. I was moving to France.

I don't know how the surviving spouse stays at home, puts a best foot forward and goes on . . . trying to live the same life in a world that is never again going to be the same. As for me, I had to escape, to get away from all the places that Mike and I had been a couple. I needed to find a new life, one that would let me keep my memories intact, but allowed me the freedom to go forward in a totally new way. Mike was right. I had to go to Paris: if only to have a plan, to know what to do next.

It would not be the same Paris dream that Mike and I had so recently shared; but it would still be Paris. The new Paris had a hard, raw edge to it. It took my breath away and made my stomach turn over. I knew it would be incredibly difficult. Could I hack it? But then, turning the question around on myself, could I hack staying at home in the suburbs of Connecticut, with a son away at school and a husband even further away? I saw my future spread out before me—long days spent writing in my office with five-P.M. trips to the Super Stop & Shop and then a whirl through Blockbuster to rent a video. I would live like that forever, the days broken up only by research trips abroad for Born to Shop and maybe a press trip or two, maybe a few nights in Manhattan. A few dates. All fix-ups, all crummy. The vision was more frightening than the thought of anyone making fun of my French, of starting over in a new place, of finding a new hairdresser.

I packed and organized lists, I checked the notes that Mike had left me—instructions on what to do when he died, written in a notebook I called The Book of the Dead. I did the paperwork of the dead while mentally decorating the apartment in Paris that I planned to rent, trying to hold on to sanity, but no longer certain what sanity was. Dusty rose for the living room, right? Yeah, sounded good.

The plan was a simple one: I would keep our house in Westport, Connecticut, and use some of the life insurance money to stake myself to a year in Paris to test the waters. Paris was going to be more of an experiment than a destination. If it didn't work out, I knew I could go back "home." Paris was just the first step toward finding stability. In the most secret parts of my brain I feared that I would wake up one morning in France and say to myself, "What the hell am I doing here? I don't even speak decent French."

I did not have second thoughts about the plan, but, well, I was a little nervous. All right, I *did* have second thoughts. I had third and fourth thoughts. In fact, I was thinking way too much. The small part of my brain that was functioning normally reminded me that visiting Paris once or twice a year and playing the role of Cinderella was a lot different from living someplace and settling into real life, especially without my *Prince Charmant*. I also knew that people who had been friends of ours in Paris might now abandon me as a single woman. I further knew that even with friends who remained true, I couldn't expect constant attention and invitations; that people would often be unavailable. I knew that to do this well, I had to be prepared to make it on my own in Paris.

I decided to do a quickie test run with a little twist to it, to make sure I would be strong enough to really make the leap that seemed so attractive from the dream-come-true perspective. I bought myself one of those JFK-CDG winter-wonder fares for less money than it costs to go to Los Angeles. I went to Paris and told no one I knew there that I was coming. I gave up my swirl of dinner dates at posh restaurants, meetings with glam friends, long meals with longer still glasses of wine with chefs and foodies, friends and business contacts. I spent a cold, wet, gray week in a tourist hotel across the street from a McDonald's in one of the less-than-chic arrondissements—alone.

It was fabulous. Paris in the rain was better than anything at home. I tested myself as best as I could.

I ate all my meals alone. I watched only Francophone television. I walked and walked and bought bouquets of flowers and sometimes went to the grocery store, not to the take-out department, but to look at the selection of real groceries. I did my usual Born to Shop browsing, but this time not for a revision of one of my books, but to price towels and bed linen. As the Born to Shop lady, I could have told you right off the bat not to buy towels or sheets in France, but my perspective was always one of a shopper returning to a home in the United States. As an American living in Paris, I needed to know the whys to the buying process. Since towels at Galeries Lafayette were priced at sixty dollars per unit, my professional sensibilities were confirmed. Towels would come from a discount store in America, where I could get a whole set for two people for less than sixty dollars. Point taken, check mark. Good work, kid.

I tried to speak only French. I didn't get as dressed up as I usually did when in Paris but instead often wore the same outfits, or parts of them, for days in a row . . . as I might at home. I wore no makeup. I gave up the Cinderella thing and became *Cendrillon de Paris*, which I hoped was the French version of Cinderella in front of the hearth, and not an ashtray.

One morning I was out walking around the soggy streets and passed a café—just your average Parisian, one on every corner kind of café. I peered inside to see if I wanted to go in, to get out of the rain, to daydream about the dusty rose living room. As my eyes swept the front portion of the café, I saw a middle-aged woman at a bistro table, alone, her reading glasses on the tabletop with her half-full cup. She was writing in a notebook.

Yes, I thought when I saw her, *yes, I can do that too*. I remembered a dinner in Paris the previous fall, right before we found out Mike was sick, a dinner when everything in the world seemed perfect, even the service. I was with Walter Wells, managing editor of the *International Herald Tribune* in Paris. I was telling him stories about my Home Stay—I had signed up to live with a French family so that I could improve my French.

I had dreamed they would be a perfect French family and teach me how to be a little more French so that when I did finally move to France, I would know how to work the oven and perform triage on the garbage. Instead, they were followers of the far-right politician Jean-Marie Le Pen: they hated Jews, Arabs and blacks . . . and also the English, but they wanted to be paid in cash so they didn't have to report the income on their taxes. At night, they locked me in my room. It was so horrible, it was funny.

"I hope you're writing this all down," Walter, always the editor, said to me.

I looked again at the woman in the café and thought of Walter. Then I walked right over to Monoprix and bought myself a set of Clairefontaine notebooks, the traditional notebook of a French schoolchild. I got four, one for each season of the coming year I would spend in Paris.

 *Winter*

Café Angelina, Galeries Lafayette, 9e
Pour boire: chocolat chaud

I moved to Paris in mid-February, six weeks after my husband died. To get myself up and out each day, and to have a home base that wasn't a hotel room or a sparsely furnished apartment, I set up "headquarters" in the Café Angelina on the third floor of the department store Galeries Lafayette.

This is not the main branch of Angelina, the famous tearoom on the rue de Rivoli which has been serving the eternal team of grandmother and granddaughter for more than a century. I like the "big" Angelina, but it is a tourist trap, and it wasn't as near to my hotel as Galeries Lafayette.

Besides, they were polite to me at the Galeries Angelina.

I went there midmorning every day, sometimes I went several times in a day. I read the paper or leafed through real-estate magazines, got off my feet, warmed up my toes and wrote in my notebook. On the cover of the first notebook I wrote: THE RUNAWAY WIDOW. *That notebook became my lifeline to starting over. I wasn't certain if I had run away, but I was forever pleased that I had the opportunity to move to Paris.*

1

I arrived at the Hotel Concorde St. Lazare on February 14 with six suitcases of essential supplies: things I had priced in January on my recon trip, things that made more sense to bring from the United States. These were mostly items I already owned and had stored in the attic, or things that I bought in U.S. discount sources after my January trip when I realized it was smarter—and cheaper—to bring the basics with me.

In these suitcases were some of the sticker-shock items I had priced in Paris and household goods that I didn't care whether I brought back to the United States or not: the old duvet that Mike had spilled ink on that I had retired to the hall closet; the somewhat washed-out navy towels with our son, Aaron's, name-tags on them from summer camp; an extra dust ruffle from when Mike came home, looked at my redecorating efforts and said, "You're kidding, right? You expect me to sleep with all those damn flowers?"

That one advance-planning trip to Paris taught me that over-weight luggage was a better bargain than buying everything from scratch at French retail prices. While I wanted a chic and stylish apartment, I was still in the experimental mode and didn't want to waste money needlessly. There were things in my base-ment at home that would do just fine. In fact, these items were happy to leave my musty basement and take on a new life in the Hotel Concorde St. Lazare.

I originally discovered this hotel for Born to Shop readers. The Concorde St. Lazare is one of my best secret-find hotels;

not as swanky as the well-known palace hotels; looked down on by visitors who disdain four star hotels, tour groups and herds of non-English-speaking foreigners. Nonetheless, the hotel is a French landmark, owned by the same team that owns the Hotel de Crillon (which means you get tons of Annick Goutal bathroom amenities) and is walking distance from all the major department stores. It has a marvelous lobby, a restored billiard room that should be a museum and rooms that are nicely decorated in the traditional hotel style of the Belle Époque. They gave me a good rate because it was February, I was a regular customer and they have long-term rates. I didn't expect to stay for too long of a long-term; my son would be arriving in three weeks and he fully expected to stay in our new apartment, not a hotel.

The hotel was one of the original train station hotels built in Victorian times; there are many of them in London and they are now being rehabbed as the latest fashion. There aren't as many in Paris and this hotel was renovated years ago. It was created in style, but before fashion.

I stayed there, I liked it, I became friendly with the then general manager, Nicolas, who turned out to be an invaluable source of information for my apartment hunt. He sat down with me daily, poured me Taittinger champagne, and marked a map of Paris with the *quartiers* (neighborhoods) he thought would best suit me. He said I needed good transportation and a good street market; for me, he liked the ninth and the seventeenth.

I had been apartment hunting in Paris once before, way back in maybe 1982, when my sister-in-law Judith lived in Paris. She was sent over on a Fulbright, jumped ship and stayed on to become a famous French playwright. She died in Paris in 1988. I remembered our house-hunting detail by detail because it was so shocking; it made me feel so dirty, partly because the apartments we looked at were dirty. They were filthy. The whole experience was so far from my concept of what French style was or should be that I felt terribly *Américaine* and utterly naïve. The first time I walked into a vacant Parisian apartment, I felt deep inside me that some terrible mistake had been made, I had that same sinking feeling you got the first time someone explained sex to you. "No! It's not possible!"

No one rented an apartment in this condition, I thought, as I followed Judy around what was to me barely an apartment. It was a tenement with a Paris zip code. You could hear Bette Davis's voice echo "What a dump!"

There were no appliances, no kitchen cupboards, no light-bulbs or light fixtures, just some dangling wires poking out of peeling-plaster walls. The century-old *ciment* tiles in the floors were chipped and rutted, wallpaper had been painted over until it buckled—where there *was* wallpaper. There were holes and ruts in the parquet. Often the apartments had a toilet without a toilet seat. It goes without saying that there were no towel racks, no systems for dispensing toilet paper or even one of those plastic pop-in paper towel racks. I was also offended by bare pipes and open spaces filled with balloon water tanks. Both are common in Paris apartments, even chic apartments—very few people ever think to box their pipes or their radiators.

Having seen these apartments prepared me somewhat for the adventure to come almost twenty years later. Social visits to France in intervening years had also helped teach me the ways of the French apartment, so that I did not completely freak out at how vastly different it was from being in a hotel . . . or from looking at apartments in the United States. When I moved into a tony apartment in Manhattan, when I was about twenty-four, my mother came to see my triumph and sniffed suspiciously that she could not believe it did not come with carpet and drapes. She would faint dead away to know that Parisian apartments often didn't come with a toilet seat.

2

So I wasn't a total debutante (which in French actually means beginner or even greenhorn), I just wasn't as sophisticated as I thought. I knew quite a few basics, such as the fact that electricity in France runs at 220 volts, different from the 110 volts used in the United States, making it necessary to buy a new TV, microwave, etcetera. I knew that even in a kitchen which was advertised as *équipée,* it might not offer a full selection of basics—an *équipée* kitchen could have a stove and oven and a dishwasher, yet no refrigerator (*frigo*). *Equipée* was in the mind of the proprietor, not the beholder.

I also had friends who gave me advice. I was told that for security I wanted a concierge, whom I quickly learned was now referred to as a *gardienne.* Then I learned:

- Tuesday was the best day to look at the rental ads in the newspaper *Le Figaro.*
- How to convert size to square meters, since all real estate in France was advertised and discussed in terms of square meters. A really nice-sized hotel room measured thirty-five to forty square meters; this was also the size of a large Paris studio apartment. On the

other hand, I have seen a really nice one-bedroom flat at forty-five square meters. It was clearly tricky.

- Where to buy appliances—Darty—because they gave the best guarantees and customer service, a concept that has not been very strong in French retail.
- To estimate rental fees, on a ballpark basis only, I learned to figure approximately €150–200 per square meter. This was a rather low estimate, given the recent rise in real estate prices in France, but it was enough to get going. It was easy enough to do the math to figure the dollar price. I soon found a direct correlation between location, condition of the building and price, so that I ended up looking at apartments that were more in the range of two hundred euros per square meter.

I knew about digicodes—the security system that kept doors locked unless you knew the precise code (changed more or less annually, just to throw off your friends, your visitors and local thieves). I also knew about door buzzers, automatic light switches on timers to save electricity, various and assorted stairwells that branch off courtyards and may or may not be visibly marked. I was afraid of cage elevators, but could operate one. In no time after that, I learned that ugly, beat-up doors often hid wonderful courtyards and even more wonderful apartments, and that ugly gravel and a boring courtyard meant nothing about the apartments inside, which were often magnificent.

I soon learned that French apartments were not advertised by the number of bedrooms—in France, anything goes—but by the number of main rooms, called *pièces*. This meant a *trois pièce* was a two bedroom apartment. The kitchen and bathroom were not counted as *pièces*.

I found my first look-see by accident. I was on the rue Marbeuf at the hairdresser and spotted the sign across the street. The rue Marbeuf is one of those magical "I-can't-believe-I-live-in-Paris" streets. It juts off the Champs Elysées; there is a metro stop (Franklin Roosevelt); there is a Monoprix dime store with grocery store at this corner—and this is the famous Monoprix which is open until ten P.M. in winter and midnight in summer. In the two to three block length of this street there's everything you could want or need, including many famous restaurants. The street has its own energy and magic along with a zip code of 75008—to me, the best of Paris.

The apartment was a tiny one bedroom, therefore called an *une pièce*, with forty-two square meters, almost five hundred square feet. The monthly rent was one thousand dollars. It was a terrific deal price-wise, but way too small for me on a full-time basis since I needed to work at home. There's no question I could have lived there comfortably, or even two people could have lived there if they were twenty-two years old, but to be there all day and night was a little too much. The possibility of guests was eliminated in such a small space. Besides, I wanted something more grand, more of a statement, like "Hey look World, I have arrived; I live in Paris!"

The shadow of my son moved with me across Paris. I felt guilty that I had abandoned him, terrified he would resent that I had moved to Paris. Despite the fact that he was six foot five inches tall and a sophomore in college, he was still my little boy. I wanted an apartment that he too could consider home.

The look-see taught me that I was looking for a large one-bedroom apartment, or even a small two-bedroom apartment of about seventy to eighty square meters. Once I knew what size would fit my needs, and my son's, I could prowl in earnest. I found that in my case, it was not a question of "where did I want to live in Paris?" but what were the most essential things I needed in a location to make life easier and smarter.

Because I had been in Paris for what I call "the big *grève*" (the strike to end all strikes when transportation came to a total halt in December 1995), I wanted to be able to walk to major parts of Paris in case of another transportation strike, since strikes are part of life in France. I wanted a metro station close to my apartment, not blocks away. It rains a lot in Paris in the winter. I didn't want to have to trudge through puddles to get to the metro.

I wanted a good bus system. At that time, I was frightened of the RER regional train system because of its complicated codes that I found too difficult to grasp, so I didn't even know what a blessing it would be to have a nearby RER station. I thought a taxi rank nearby would be smart . . . and also a grocery store, or one of those minimart things that are open when no one else is open. I wanted to be close enough to the highway to get to the airport without going broke on taxi fares. I also wanted calm and sunlight and a wonderful psychological float that made you sigh and say, "Yes, I *do* live in Paris."

Although I love the Marais and in particular the place Ste. Catherine, the word *marais* means swamp in French. The Marais is considered more humid in the summer, and wreaks havoc on naturally curly hair. If I rejected Florida for fear of bad hair days, the Marais would also be out. What a pity.

While tourists know the Marais as the home of the Picasso Museum and the magnificent place des Vosges or as a good shopping street where stores are open on Sundays, I equate it with the place Ste. Catherine—a secret square known only by a few insiders that is more like an Italian piazza than a French *place*. It's small, with cafés and restaurants and surrounding townhouses filled with apartments. To me, it is one of the most desirable places on the Right Bank. But alas, Saint Catherine must not have had curly hair.

I began to go to real estate agencies in my choice neighborhoods (the eighth, ninth and seventeenth arrondissements), working from a printout of addresses from the general manager of the Concorde St. Lazare. These three choices were made from my knowledge of Paris, with the help of maps of Paris, the metro and the city's best street markets. As much as I love to visit the Left Bank, I am not really a Left Bank kind of person. My regular hotels, aside from the Concorde St. Lazare (located at the edge of the eighth), were in the area between the first and the eighth arrondissements. I would have looked for a place to live in the first, but it's dead on Sundays and not great for supermarkets and real life, unless you happen to live within a block of Monoprix Opéra.

Friends told me the best way to find a place was to simply walk the streets in the districts that I was interested in, to talk to all the real estate agents and to concierges if possible. There are scads of agencies in Paris, all strung with enticing photos and notices in their front windows—sort of the real estate equivalent of puppies frolicking in the window of a pet shop.

Paris real estate agencies do not have multiple listings. This is because Paris is essentially a city of tiny villages. Real estate agents have long argued that they were local experts who best sold their own neighborhoods and only their own neighborhoods. I eventually went to about fifty different agencies.

The first agency I visited was in the ninth. There was only one person in the agency at that time. I told him that I didn't speak French very well, but I would try my best and that I needed to rent an apartment. He understood me, laughed kindly and said my French was a lot better than his English; there was no problem. Who ever said the French were rude? That Parisians disdained Americans?

I told him what I was looking for; he had just the thing. *Voilà!* He showed me a photo of the front of the building (typical Haussmannian style) and the printed architectural floor plan. The apartment was considerably larger and cheaper than my wildest expectations—eighty-six square meters with a rent of $1,200, considerably below my budget of $1,500. Furthermore, it was on the top floor, which meant lots of sunlight. Part of living in Paris must be sitting in the rooms of your flat and watching the sunlight play through the windows and across the rooftops, *n'est-ce pas?* There was an elevator in the building. I made an appointment.

The place was frankly fabulous—nicer and larger than I had ever dreamed of: a full dining room and separate living room, two bedrooms, a *dressing* as they say, or walk-in closet as we say. There was a gentle flow to the space; you could close your eyes and envision your first dinner party. The interior of the building itself was nice enough but not anything to brag about; the elevator was acceptable—small and creaky, but you could giggle and call it charming. With all this space and light, this one was a winner and a true steal.

Of course there was a catch. The block in which the building was situated was, well, it was the pits. It was beyond ugly or without charm. It was flat out disgusting. It was embarrassing. It was downright depressing. You would have felt sorry for me if you came to visit. I felt sorry for me just thinking about living there. The building had a discount wedding shop in the downstairs retail space, with an acre of shining polyester wedding gowns and dull powder-blue tuxedos on very dead-looking mannequins from the 1960s. Most of the other storefronts on the block were closed; out of business. The few that were open just made the impression stronger of how financially depressed this block was and how depressing it would be to live there. If I was going to live my dream year in a dream city, I did not want to live in the most underachieving block in Paris.

3

On the phone, a broker told me about an apartment near the metro Villiers, which had become my number one choice of neighborhood. (It's on the borderline between the eighth and the seventeenth, with an excellent, two-store Monoprix at the corner and a good metro station.) The apartment was exactly what I wanted: a stunning, gorgeous, chic, fabulous, two-bedroom, drop-dead wonderful apartment that would make you weep with envy and delight, high ceilings and moldings included, and bigger than what I was looking at: a full one hundred square meters.

The price was five hundred dollars per month more than my budget, or about two thousand dollars per month. I refused to go look at it. I told the broker I wanted the same apartment for less money and asked him to keep looking for me. He told me I would never find what I wanted for less, even in a lesser neighborhood. I thought he was just doing what real estate brokers do, trying to frighten me in order to trade me up, to get me to pay more.

It took me a week to come to the conclusion that he was right . . . and I did want a safe neighborhood. I had seen that depressing apartment in the ninth. It was time to learn my lessons, to grow up. Of course, by the time I put all this together in my head, the Villiers apartment he had raved about was rented. Many apartments were bought or rented within seconds of the arrival of the prospective tenant.

I was not that sharp in those first weeks. I finally decided to raise the rent-per-month bar and go for the whole fantasy, the nice two-bedroom apartment, one I would be pleased to live in, even if it meant taking an extra six thousand dollars from the life insurance money. After all, I was only going to be in Paris for one year, so it might as well be a very nice year. Besides, what would two thousand dollars a month buy me in Manhattan? A studio? A studio in a bad neighborhood without a doorman or a Monoprix? The comparison gave me great comfort.

I stood taller; I smiled more often—I was pleased with myself and the decision. I was going to live like Catherine Deneuve.

4

Before I arrived in Paris, my girlfriend Pascale-Agnès—who had been teaching me French survival tips for twenty years and has been my Born to Shop assistant since the series began—gave me the list of paperwork I would need in order to rent a flat. She warned me that I would not be allowed to rent an apartment for any price other than one-quarter of my monthly salary. I found this disturbing since I had no salary that year—I had taken a leave from Born to Shop while I nursed my husband—and was living off life insurance money he left me.

I had in hand a dossier created to properly present myself to my prospective landlord; I brought copies of Mike's and my income tax returns for the past three years; I had copies of bank statements in the United States and in France, as well as copies of the life insurance papers. I had a Born to Shop book plus a Born to Shop press kit, the international version that has articles about me in French, German and British. I had a letter of recommendation in French and on letterhead from Walter Wells of the *International Herald Tribune.* I thought I was prepared.

Along with all the U.S. bank and insurance information, I had statements from my French bank. Mike's sister had died in Paris, leaving all her worldly goods (as they say) to Mike. It didn't make sense to close her bank account and send the money to the United States, as we would have lost a great deal on the exchange. So we kept the account, added to it every now and then and used it to pay our bills in France when we went to visit. When Mike died, I inherited this bank account. Surely a future proprietor would be impressed that I had a long-standing account in France. Surely a proprietor would understand some version of "widow of independent means."

A first apartment was always hard, but the organized person—and one who made it clear he had money in the bank—could prevail. Of this I was certain. Lafayette, I am here. *Voilà.*

5

I continued to make the rounds in search of a place to live. I read newspapers and marked them up with a neon pink felt-tip pen, then I walked up and down the streets of my chosen arrondissements, stopping at the windows at each *immoblier,* or real estate agency. One day I saw a promising ad in the newspaper and rushed out to see an apartment at Villiers. The concierge took one look at me and announced that she would not even show me the apartment. I wouldn't like it; it wasn't nice enough for me. Why should we waste our time?

Then she whispered the terrible secrets that lay beyond: it was on the ground floor with a mezzanine . . . and it was dark. These are the two greatest sins in French apartment dwelling: thou shalt not live on the ground or first floor (read Diane Johnson's novel *Le Mariage*); thou shalt assume a Paris apartment is dark unless you see the light yourself or unless it is on the top floor. Dark is bad.

My girlfriend Marie-Jo—whom I met when we traded houses back in 1984—suggested that I move into her *chambre de bonne* and take my time while looking for an apartment. Most people I knew in Paris told me it took months, or years, to find an apartment. I went over to Marie-Jo's fancy neighborhood overlooking one of the Seine canals and looked at the *chambre de bonne*.

A *chambre de bonne* is the maid's room, built into the eaves of a mansard roof; when you buy an apartment, you get the *chambre de bonne* with the sale or are allowed to buy it. In some buildings the elevator goes to this floor; in other buildings you take the elevator to the top floor and then walk up either a half or full flight of stairs. The *chambre de bonne* usually measures nine or ten square meters, less than one hundred square feet. Unless it is renovated, it does not have a toilet and may not have any running water whatsoever. Parts of the room may be too shallow for a tall person like me to stand up in because the space is always in the eaves of the roof.

With pride at being able to help me out, Marie-Jo showed me her *chambre de bonne,* which was currently being used as a TV room for her teenage children. It had a trundle bed in it and a

TV set (no cable). It had a window the size of the porthole on a cruise ship. It was fine as a spare room in the attic for the kids to watch TV; for a grieving widow whose life had just been turned upside down, it was pathetic. There wasn't a lick of paint, wall-paper, curtains or charm. Sure I could have fixed it up and sold the "before-and-after" pictures to *Elle Décoration* magazine, but it wasn't my apartment and it would have insulted my friend if I had asked if I could decorate. I scanned the room and tried to think of something nice to say. Oh, I told her, it was charming, just like Van Gogh's room in his famous painting. I thought I too would kill myself if I had to live in that room for too long. In fact, historians may want to reconsider Van Gogh's motive for suicide.

6

Then suddenly, good luck: an announcement from a friend who had been cold calling brokers for me. He was French and obvi-ously spoke French better than I (actually, just about anyone speaks French better than I do). He had found something that met my needs on avenue Wagram (say Vah-grahm), just one metro stop past Villiers and not terribly far from where Walter and Patricia Wells lived then. I raced over there for a rendezvous with the broker.

There was a tiny café across the street; a convenience store on the corner; a dry cleaner, bakery and video store down the block. The building itself was not Haussmannian but more fed-eral: red brick with white trim, small and folksy. There were white lace curtains on the windows of the front door; there was a *gardienne* office to the left and a tiny box elevator that brought you to the top floor. There was only one apartment on each floor; the wood on the staircase that encircled the elevator cage had the patina of thousands of feet over hundreds of years. Oriental-style runner carpets were held in place by heavy and highly polished brass bars. It was elegant and charming and very French, without being too fancy or *de trop*. It felt like me.

The apartment totaled ninety square meters, which included the space on the balconies, as is common practice in French math. This meant the apartment was closer to eighty square meters: it had two bedrooms, a large bathroom with an enormous old-fashioned bathtub and room for both a washer and a dryer—which the tenant had to provide. The toilet was in a separate water closet; there was a *dressing* and each bedroom had its own closet. Not real closets, but IKEA style built-ins. Still, for Paris that was very lucky. I couldn't stop grinning. The earth was beginning to move.

The kitchen was very small and not *équipée*—it had a sink, but nothing else. The broker did not speak English yet we still managed to engage in a heated discussion as to what went where in the kitchen. I had a small panic attack that there was no room for a stove—that the apartment was meant to have a two-burner hot plate instead, as I have seen in many Paris apartments. A hot plate was a deal breaker. We eventually got the logistics worked out, the broker realized she had confused the plugs and wires and spigots; I breathed a delighted sigh.

The rent on the apartment was $1,700 with another $150 per month in building charges. I was advised that it would cost approximately $3,000 to equip the kitchen. In a three-year lease, the savings in rent between $1,700 and $2,000 covered the cost of the kitchen after a year and a half . . . and I would own the kitchen equipment. On the other hand, I only planned to stay for a year and had no idea what I would do with French kitchen equipment in 220 volts.

I told the broker that I was seriously interested and would return the next day with a friend who spoke French and English. I returned with Pascale-Agnès, who arrived in her regular uniform—a twin sweater set and pearls, velvet hair band, Hermès scarf and a neat little designer handbag hung on her wrist. She took a quick look around and nodded her assent. She paid it her highest compliment, "This apartment is exactly what my mother should be living in."

I said I would take it and passed over my financial dossier to the broker while I floated down the street. I announced to anyone who would listen that I had found my dream apartment, further pointing out that you could stand on the balcony and actually see the Arc de Triomphe. I asked a friend in the United States to send over some of my bordeaux-colored things to match the rose-colored carpets. It never occurred to me that anything could or would go wrong. I was naïve.

The following day, the broker called back to ask me numerous financial questions. Did I work in France? No. Did I have a *carte de séjour* (permit to stay or to work in France)? No. Would someone in France sign the lease to guarantee it for me? No.

Okay, the apartment was mine if I put a *caution* (deposit) of three years' rent (approximately $70,000) in the account of the owner of the apartment. All legal leases in France are for three years. The owner would have access to the money and I would not. Not only did I go nuts with rage and indignation, but I asked other American friends about this practice to see if it was normal. They all admitted that getting their first apartment had been a bitch, that either someone had signed for them or they had paid the *caution*——sums that were never returned or that required legal action to gain access to. No one, however, had heard of a three-year *caution*.

Two days later, the broker announced that the owner had eased up: she would accept a one-year caution, but would keep the interest earned during the three years of the lease. I actually thought about it for a few minutes before I walked out of the deal, heartbroken.

Pascale-Agnès and I went to see another apartment; this one proposed by another broker, a man who was supposed to show me a flat at Parc Monceau, a very nice residential area adjacent to Villiers and also near the Wells's apartment. The broker was unable to get the keys to the Monceau apartment, however, and therefore decided, on his own accord, to show me an apartment at place Pereire, two blocks north of Monceau. This information was communicated to us by mobile phone five minutes prior to our date at the Monceau address. I had no idea where or what Pereire was; I kept calling it Perrier, like the bottled water. (Say Pair-Air, not Perry-A.)

The place Pereire is a large circular garden, planted with roses of all colors, that anchors an *étoile* (star) of some eight different streets. To the west is the Arc de Triomphe, just three blocks away; to the north, the highway to the airport. There is both a metro stop and a separate RER station; there are four good bus lines. In short, the fact that I had never heard of this area just meant that I was uninformed.

The building itself was gorgeous, with enormous wrought iron gates over the front entrance and the initials AG gilted into the gates: my son's initials. The entryway was even more stunning.

The stained glass looked new, but was a sensational touch. This possibility was far more fancy than the one I had tried to rent; the building was truly in grand standing. I grew even taller. You mean I could live in a building like this one? I'd had no idea.

The apartment itself was big, but not perfect. It was what a New Yorker calls a railroad flat—the rooms all ran off a very, very long (and dark) hallway. It was a back apartment, on a courtyard, with an ugly view of the garbage dump of another building from most of the back windows. Hey, I lived in New York for twenty years; I knew a bad apartment when I saw one.

There were balconies overlooking the building's courtyard adjoining each of the three principal rooms; each terrace was overgrown with moss and algae. There was *beaucoup de* pigeon poop. Pascale-Agnès said this was a bad sign, indicating a humidity problem (my hair!) and the possibility of disease from sick pigeons. But the ceilings in the rooms were very high; most of the walls had molding and curlicues and rosettes; there were marble fireplaces in each of the three main rooms and crackly old mirrors that made my ass look smaller. The kitchen was enormous, even by American standards. By French standards, it was a miracle.

The apartment measured one hundred square meters; the rent was $1,800 and the monthly charges were $165, making the total around $2,000 a month. There were good parts and bad parts to this apartment; no emotion washed over me except fatigue. I had really loved the Wagram apartment, the one that got away. I could not fall in love again so quickly.

The broker asked if I was interested. Pascale-Agnès was not interested at all and urged me to flee . . . and quickly. I told the broker my problem with having lost an apartment that I adored because I have international revenue but do not work in France. He said he didn't think that would be a problem with this proprietor because he was German, the director general of the French division of a German stocking and pantyhose firm.

. Pascale-Agnès and I retreated to the corner café; we drank hot chocolate and perhaps I cried. We were agreed that it was not a perfect apartment, but that the extra space was nice and the three fireplaces were extra nice. We decided to do a tour of the neighborhood, as we were now three metro stops from Villiers and in Indian territory, as far as I knew. Was I still in Paris?

When I spotted a branch of Monoprix on the next block, the quandary suddenly was resolved—my future was clear; I knew I had arrived. We immediately returned to the café, we called the broker from Pascale-Agnès's mobile phone and told him that if the proprietor would accept international income and my dossier, I would take the apartment. My heart was not in it, but I needed to take an apartment and feared that if I waited for one that I loved, I could lose this one too. Besides, the idea of a Monoprix just a few hundred meters from my door was *ciel* (heaven).

Within two hours I was told that I was accepted by the man I soon began to call (behind his back) Herr Strumpf, the German pantyhose king. I was directed to come to the real estate agency the next day to pay the fees and get the keys. Then I ordered a second hot chocolate—this time a *chocolat viennois,* hot chocolate with whipped cream—and began to daydream about the décor. Maybe Wedgwood blue for the living room, not dusty rose? Should I ship over the blue-and-white Spode dishes or were they in fact too English for France?

7

I couldn't imagine that a French real estate agency could be any worse than a New York one, so I felt no fear. I just wanted the keys in my hand and a chance to start measuring. Yes, said the broker, the apartment was about to be mine; yes, I could have the keys immediately. There were just a few technicalities, however:

1) Although it was the end of February and I did not even see the apartment beforehand, I was told that I could have it retroactively to February 15 or I could wait until March 15. Since my son, Aaron, was arriving March 6; I chose February 15. I fought on this point, but I did not fight hard enough. I actually didn't care at that point. I just needed it to be settled so that I could move on to the next step. I was prepared to write a big check to get in and the fact that I was being cheated out of two weeks' worth of rent was of small consequence.

2) The apartment needed painting. The previous tenants had been there for only a year and a half, but they smoked constantly so the *blanc cassé* (off-white) walls were disgusting. I was told I could have one month's rent as a credit against the fee of the painting, but I was to pay for the painting and to contract it out and supervise the work. The estimates to paint the

three main rooms without kitchen or bathrooms—
not including ceilings, trims or moldings—ran from
$3,000 to $4,000. Since this was more than a month's
rent, I failed to see the advantage to me, but I was
too dazed to care and I knew I couldn't paint the
apartment myself.

3) I was to write a check for three months' rent as a security deposit; I paid the one half month's rent from
March 15 to April 1 per the painting barter plan; I
additionally paid a finder's fee to the agency of
$1,750—a total that was derived from some specific
mathematical equation that equaled not quite one
month's rent. In short, it cost about $10,000 in cash
to get into the apartment.

A set of strange keys were placed in my hand. I squeezed
them against my itching palms until the sharp points hurt my
hand and their cold metal grew warm.

I had signed the three-year lease, which could be legally broken with written notice three months before intent to vacate. If
I was transferred to another city for work, I could leave with
one month's notice. When I did vacate the apartment, it was to
be in the exact condition I found it in. I would pay for anything
that had to be fixed from the deposit I had left. Meanwhile, anything I added to the apartment would be at my expense and
would then have to be undone before I left. Even curtain rods. I
began to wonder if I would have to start smoking just to get the
walls back to their previous condition.

My three-year lease was actually up after two and a half years
when it automatically renewed itself for another three years. At

the end of this two-and-a-half-year period, the proprietor had the right to take back the apartment or to raise the rent by 3 percent. I would know for sure on August 15. It was suddenly clear to me why August 15 is known as the Feast of the Assumption. I had to *assume* I could stay there.

8

Napoléon was the hero of, you should excuse the expression, the little man. I don't mean short, I mean the real person, the guy in the *rue*, the one who had no famous last name or aristocratic connections and therefore was most likely to get screwed by the system. In order to protect this guy, Napoléon came up with a series of laws and contracts based on there being pieces of paper with everything written down and plenty of copies of these papers, so who had what rights could not be disputed. With Napoléon's new systems, Monsieur or Madame Anyone had unheard-of protection and in case of misunderstandings, could whip out their own copy of the document to prove their point. This meant a whole new world of rights for mankind, and a whole new meaning to paperwork. And this was before photocopy machines.

This need for lots of papers and for enormous files created a large civil servant population and a group of bureaus that could barely function because of all the paper and the old-fashioned ways of doing things. To make sure that everyone was treated the same (the basic tenet of Napoleonic law), nothing could be revised, updated or changed because that would be unfair to the others. In fact, the civil code has only been changed twice since Napoléon created it.

When I signed the lease, although I could not read a word of it, I had to write *lu et approuvé* at the bottom of each page: read and approved. This would hold up against me in court, if I tried to say I didn't know what I was doing. (Thanks, Bonaparte.) But there were rituals in place that would also protect me.

9

After all the money had been paid, the paperwork read and approved and the keys exchanged, Pascale-Agnès, her husband, Thierry, the real estate broker and I returned to the flat to make the inspection. This is a very big deal by French law, sort of a "speak now or forever hold your peace" situation with many legal implications. The idea is that everyone agrees on the existing condition of the apartment before it changes hands, so it's clear what damage the tenant has caused when he vacates.

I did not understand what constituted normal wear and tear after a three-year or six-year lease on a 125-year-old apartment or who was responsible for what, but I figured whatever it was, it would end up being my fault. I hadn't lived in France very long, but I have traveled for many years for Born to Shop, and I knew that when you are doing business in a foreign country, the American was always the one who was wrong. This is a good rule to understand upfront in any situation when you are a guest in a foreign country.

The inspection itself was very thorough and took sheaves of

paper and official forms that had to be signed by both parties: the proprietor and the lessee. Since I didn't even know the word for "hall" in French, I wasn't of too much help. In my opinion, even though I have survived the jungles of New York and do understand nuance, the apartment was fine, it needed painting, that was all. I wasn't crazy about having to pay for the painter myself, but there was no question that the walls were a disturbing dirty shade and the leftover pockmarks of molly screws were not attractive. Besides, it was curious to wonder if the previous tenants had had a mirror on the ceiling in the bedroom. Just what was attached to those holes up there on the side of the molding to the far right corner? Surely no chandelier went there. Perhaps a trapeze?

The French team did it the French way: the old fine-tooth comb inspection. Pascale-Agnès and her husband are both university professors. Pascale-Agnès is very aristocratic and French, but has a feisty side to her. She went to law school, so she will argue with someone when she knows she is right. Her husband is very shy, but sharp-eyed and detail oriented. Together they are a formidable team.

Every scratch in the mirror, missing one-inch chunk in the parquet, and buckle in the wall was noted in detail. The official preprinted chart—there is (bien sûr) a specific French piece of paperwork that must be completed for this inspection—was filled with tiny script and included three pages of forms. Pascale-Agnès explained to me that this paperwork had to be done as carefully as possible, otherwise an unscrupulous landlord could blame the tenant—and charge accordingly—for all sorts of damages that had already existed. She even taught me that there is a profession of people (les huissiers) who make a living by inspecting apartments and goods—they are used in rentals, sales, deaths and divorces—because their so-called impartial judgment holds up in court better than any "he-said-she-said" dialog.

At the completion of the paperwork, I packed up all my stuff and prepared to move. I hired a taxi driver with a van, checked out of the hotel, had all my coats in my arms and was waiting for the driver when my portable phone rang and a man who introduced himself as Herr Strumpf—my new landlord—suggested that we get together. I explained it wasn't a very good time for me; I was moving into his flat at that very moment and the van was waiting downstairs.

"*Nein,*" he announced. "We will meet for our mutual benefit. My driver is taking me to where you are. Where are you?"

His English was smooth, fluent and almost lyrical but he was quite firm. As I saw it, once again the Hun had us Frenchies up against the wall. So there in the lobby of the Concorde St. Lazare, with my winter coats piled up all around me, the van driver cooling his heels while he let the meter run, I held court and gave Herr Strumpf his audience.

Herr Strumpf was not at all what I expected him to be, no kindly old gray-haired, red-nosed, corpulent uncle he. He was strikingly handsome, short, small-bodied and well dressed. He soon proved to be a nasty little man with a mean streak as he whipped out the inspection sheet. He curtly announced there was nothing wrong with his apartment and that I could not move in because of the way the forms had been completed, with so many pages of details and such elaborate descriptions of faults. He renounced the signed lease, said I should pay a *caution* or we would call the whole thing off.

The moment remains frozen in my memory bank even now. The options open to me in that second spun faster than Vanna White's Wheel of Fortune could have ever imagined. I thought about crying. I thought about throwing myself at his feet, doing the wounded widow bit, begging for mercy. Mostly, I thought about having to move back into the hotel, unpack and start all over again. I decided this was not the kind of man you played patty-cake with. I let loose with all the emotions that were heretofore restrained. I screamed at him and told him we had signed papers and he was just a little late on all counts. When I finished the tirade, he smiled at me.

"I love it when you're angry like that. Your eyes flash."

I was torn between wanting this apartment desperately and hating him because I knew there would be trouble later on, hating him because he was a German man obviously born before 1939, hating him because I had no place else to go . . . and the three fireplaces were looking better and better. I also hated myself for not having the guts to tell him to get lost.

In the end, he gave me a second set of keys, got in his chauffeured Mercedes-Benz and drove into the traffic. We had agreed to do a new inspection of the apartment together. He invited himself over for drinks a few days hence.

10

I moved into the empty apartment even before the painters arrived. I set up housekeeping in the kitchen, which was as large as my first apartment in Manhattan and was not going to be painted. There was no refrigerator or washing machine, but hell, it was February and any leftovers could be set out on the windowsill.

The electricity was already on; the phone was switched on automatically and immediately. I slept on Pascale-Agnès's beach mat and used my coat as a bedspread. I wasn't eating very much in those weeks after Mike died, so food didn't much matter, plus I had brought peanut butter (Skippy, crunchy) and jelly (Knott's Berry Farm boysenberry) with me from the States. Peanut butter and jelly on a toasted croissant is really quite good.

I rushed into the apartment because I didn't want to pay rent and a hotel room at the same time. I was on a budget: every hundred euros spent on a hotel room was a hundred euros taken from the decorating budget. Goodbye to unlimited use of electricity without worry and endless Annick Goutal soaps; hello real world.

Herr Strumpf came over to see me, as promised. He *harrumphed* when he saw my nest in the kitchen. I did not offer him a drink. We walked through the apartment, he wrote some X's on various lines in forms clutched into his gloved hands and thrust the charts at me to be signed. I signed. I was not going to look for another apartment nor move out of this one. I did not even read what was written on the pages.

I thought it would be relatively easy to get started in a Parisian apartment—a few beds from the local equivalent of Macy's and a few trips to the flea markets. Since I still owned the house in Westport, and my son had all our extra furnishings at his apartment in Boston where he attended college, I had to start from scratch—just as Mike and I had planned to do when we played the Let's Move to Paris game. In our game, it was fun.

I was wrong. I was wrong about the flea markets; wrong

about Macy's. I was wrong about how much I thought I knew about shopping in France. Well, wrong about it from a living-in-France point of view. Here I was, the Born to Shop Lady, the woman who had at that point written nine editions of *Born to Shop Paris* and who had been called the most famous shopper in the world—stumped by my own apartment, unable to even get a bed delivered. Don't tell Oprah.

There were no dining room tables at the flea market at Vanves, which I have always considered the best of the Parisian flea markets. In fact, the only big pieces of furniture I found for immediate consumption were two armchairs. Man cannot live by armchairs alone. In desperation, I came up with a new plan of attack. If all of Gaul was divided into three parts, then so was my hunting and gathering. I searched for the things I needed from three different sources:

- Hotels: many of the hotels where I had friends were undergoing renovations and possibly had furniture to sell, give away or lend out. I also knew that large hotels or hotel chains keep extra furniture in storage.
- *FUSAC*: the expatriate journal was the main communications link for those in transit. There were pages devoted to advertised tag sales hosted by those who were leaving Paris. I also knew that when I left I could resell items through *FUSAC*.
- Mass Market Stores: Junky furniture—usually in kit form—could be bought from stores like IKEA, Conforama, Habitat and even Leroy Merlin (the Home Depot of France) and could be counted on to fill in when flea markets failed me. What I've always hated about this kind of furniture is that it often costs as

much as a flea market find, but doesn't have the same quality. Still, it had some resale value in terms of *FUSAC*.

Any shopper knows that the worst shopping mistakes are made when under pressure and that you always overpay when you have to go out and buy something to meet an immediate need. So it was for me during those first two weeks of setting up housekeeping. I had imagined it was going to be so much fun. Instead, it was a dull headache filled with frustration and the sense of bleeding cash, for no good reason. I am still living with some of the shopping mistakes I made back then. I am also bearing the financial burden of having bought the same thing twice, once when I was desperate and then again when I found the one I really liked.

Part of my unease lay in the fact that I had no idea how to get around the outrageous cost of basics in France. Sure, rent and food were cheap, but a coffee grinder that cost $10 in the United States was $30 in France. A rather basic vacuum cleaner cost $300. A simple plug-in telephone? $110. A CD player, the cheap kind not the fancy kind, began at $100. I paid $400 for mine because it had both 110 and 220 volts and could be used in the United States. At that point, I thought I was only going to stay in Paris for the one year of the experiment, so it made the shopping and stocking up that much harder and the resentment over high prices more keenly felt.

I knew about Auchan, the French hypermarket that serves the suburbs of Paris and the French provinces in much the same way Target, Kmart and Wal-Mart do the United States, but the Auchan outside Paris only delivered groceries, not beds, lamps or appliances. If I wanted these items, they had to be bought in Paris at a Parisian department store and delivered on the schedule provided by the store, a rotation that went by neighborhood and arrondissement and could result in a ten-day wait if you just missed the cycle.

That left the major department stores, all of which did indeed sell household items and beds. The best for home needs has always been BHV and the beds there were known to be less expensive than at Galeries Lafayette, even though the two stores have the same parent company.

I learned that all things in France, from clothes to bed linen to *canapés* (sofabeds) to computers and even dishwasher detergent, have a promotional season and are marked down once, maybe twice a year. Locals know about these promotions or know how to research the promotions, then they wait for the sale and never, ever buy at full price. But these promotions are spaced out around the year, and last for a short window of time, at the most, three weeks. You have to know when they are coming and be willing to wait it out. You have to have an equipped home before you plan to re-equip it. I had an empty home. I could not wait and therefore had to pay full retail (oh my!) for everything.

For the most part, full retail in France is 30 percent to 50 percent higher than in the United States for the same goods or similar goods and may cost as much for items of lower quality than what you are used to at home.

The only thing that was easy and inexpensive to buy was flowers. France is a land of flowers, they spill out of containers on the street at almost every corner; they are inexpensive enough to be given to almost anyone for almost anything or to buy for yourself by the armful without it being any special occasion at all. *Les fleurs* are a piece of the fiber of French life. I decided that nothing filled an empty apartment better than fresh flowers. I knew that Mike would have agreed and bought myself flowers in his name.

My new apartment turned out to be two blocks from the place des Ternes, home of a daily flower market set up in a circular *place*, where each vendor had his own little villa of flowers and the sidewalks were a riot of color and texture. They sold plants in pots, ready-made bouquets wrapped in tissue and cut flowers, as fresh as the day and the season, priced a little higher than they should be because you were paying for the cuteness and the convenience of knowing there would always be flowers in this haven of residential rich folk.

I also lived one block from avenue de Villiers and avenue Wagram, with an entire cluster of flower shops. The guys on avenue de Villiers have what many people say are the best prices in Paris. They do a big business on Sundays, acting as the meeting place of the tony locals who are bringing flowers to Sunday luncheon with *maman* or others. The dogs are as well groomed as the women; the men have slicked back hair and crooked noses garnished with thin, graying moustaches. They wear navy blazers and jeans. They pay by house charge account. They have been represented by Maurice Chevalier and Louis Jourdan in the movies. They vote republican or royalist. They give jewelry to their mistresses.

While the furniture was slow in coming together, the mantel in the living room was always decorated with a large vase filled with fabulous flowers. My balconies also had fresh plants on them, the geraniums outside my bedroom were color coordinated with the fabrics inside my bedroom. I positioned my bed (once I had one) so that I could sit against a mass of pillows and look out over the courtyard at the flowers and the sunlight. Then I knew for sure that I lived in Paris.

11

I was running on overdrive those first days in the new apartment. I missed my husband in abstract terms only; I didn't feel sorry for myself. I was too tired. Setting up housekeeping and trying to function in a strange country in a language that was hard for me was a full-time occupation. I felt like a character in a Stephen King novel, eaten alive by an alien environment that others thought was harmless. At night I was happy to sink into my nest, watch a little TV I didn't understand and then pass out into a deep sleep. There's nothing more hypnotizing after eight P.M. than the drone of a language that makes no sense to you.

In those early days, I moved as if in a trance. I gave directions to the painters with a dictionary as an appendage to my left hand. When they tested the living room paint, at first a watery urine shade of pale yellow, I kept yelling "*plus daffodil.*" I meant *plus jonquil,* but it didn't quite come out right. I knew it was a flower something.

I wore a tape measure around my neck instead of jewelry. I dressed in jeans and one of my husband's old shirts. I resembled more the Madwoman of Chaillot than Coco Chanel.

I was operating under the influence of an antidepressant, but the strangeness of the situation pumped adrenaline throughout my body. I worked in a rush that carried me over the hump of leaving home and getting set up. I woke at six A.M. to clean. I knew I wasn't behaving normally, but then, what was normal in my situation?

Drugs didn't make me a merry widow, but I felt that I had my life in control and was doing rather well, despite the fact that I was over budget. I was pleased that I had decided to try France. Every time someone invited me to lunch or dinner, I was pleased that I had left Westport and not fallen into a widow rut. I didn't choose for my husband to die or to make this move, but given the circumstances, I felt tinges of delight that I had the opportunity to start over.

When I walked down the streets of Paris and men gave me an appreciative look, I was glad that I had chosen a city where older women were visually enjoyed—even by younger men. In America, a middle-aged woman—no matter how attractive—is invisible. Many divorced and widowed friends had told me that their social lives in the United States disappeared after the flurry of condolence-inspired social invites.

In France, being a single woman did not make you a pariah. At Parisian dinner parties, no hostess cared if there was an even number of men and women or arranged a seating plan based on boy-girl, boy-girl. Furthermore, the art of flirtation thrived in Europe so that a woman who had been married a long time and found herself single and depressed could at least enjoy a few hours of eyelash batting. Taxis drivers, black and white, Arab and French, always gave me come-on lines or asked me on dates. I was suddenly transformed from an ordinary suburban housewife into a hot number, simply by changing my zip code.

About the time that I moved to Paris there was a news story covered in the local and international press. The story compared the sex lives of the American and French population and discovered that the French didn't have more sex per week, but they had sex later into their lives. American women at age fifty often considered they were too old for a sexual relationship; not so Frenchwomen.

Maybe every American woman over fifty should move to France.

12

On a sunny and perfect March Sunday, I went to the flea market at Vanves, trying desperately to get the apartment ready for my son's first visit. I scored a bamboo and wicker chaise longue from the 1930s that I couldn't resist ($150) and a matched set of wooden and upholstered twin bed frames for the guest room ($150 the pair). I also found a drop-dead gorgeous walnut carved armoire for just under one thousand dollars. Prices at the flea market were at least fair; I beat the bargaining problem and solved the issue of furniture deliveries in one fell swoop.

"What is your best price?" I'd ask about a piece I was serious about.

When given the answer to the question, instead of bargaining any further, I simply said, "and that price includes delivery, of course?"

Although it was often done with some hesitation, the vendors agreed.

After they arrived at my apartment, I always made sure that the *brocanteurs* built or installed the furniture—as bed frames and armoires all come apart and are often put back together again with pegs rather than modern tools. In fact, as I watched them install the furniture, I wondered how it would ever be rebuilt once shipped back to America where I wasn't certain you could find tradesmen schooled in eighteenth-century arts. (To insert the peg in the hole, first place it in your mouth to moisten the sides.)

Because it was inappropriate to tip for this service, and would have added to my costs, I merely thanked each person profusely and offered up a Coca-Cola. They were all delighted. I soon learned that a free Coca-Cola can buy a lot of friends.

The wife of an old family friend came to visit me and to check on my progress—she being one of the many names on my list of people to contact in Paris. She seemed genuinely amazed at the mélange that was gathering in the apartment. She confessed to being envious that I could pick and choose my environment—from the day of her marriage she had lived in a flat bought for her by the groom's parents and furnished by her family with inherited furniture that she loathed and was forced to keep, care for and pass on to her children. She was celebrating retirement now, because she had sold the big apartment, sent the hated furniture to her children and at age seventy could finally buy what she wanted. She said she didn't care about the quality of that furniture or the family history that it represented—it was big, dark, heavy and cold and she was thrilled to have dumped it on her kids.

At least old furniture, especially older French furniture, was well made. It made buying new, instant furniture a sad case of throwing away money. Many of the young French couples go out to IKEA (on the outskirts of Paris, near the Charles de

Gaulle airport) for their furnishings, but I didn't want fake country French made from a Swedish company that provided goods in build-it-yourself kits with directions in French. I moved to Paris, I wanted French. But it wasn't going well. Shopping at a flea market is like shopping at Loehmann's—you never find what you need when you need it, you just find stuff you like.

I remembered my idea of talking to my hotelier friends. The general manager of the Meurice, whose hotel was then closed for an extravagant renovation, said the bad stuff was already gone and the rest was being refurbished. The general manager of the Four Seasons Hotel George V, which had just reopened after lengthy renovations, said he had only important antiques and that the old George V stuff had gone years ago. The general manager of the Hotel Concorde St. Lazare confessed he had a large *réserve* and invited me over.

Under the eaves of the hotel's mansard roof, running the length of the main building (a city block), nestled the *réserve*, which housed furniture not currently in use, much of it in sad shape. It was better than Ali Baba's cave, even if each piece was marked with a room number on its bottom or back side. I was given two twin beds as a gift of the house (*Bienvenue à Paris*) and allowed to borrow whatever else I wanted with the sole obligation to restore any piece I took and to return it when I left Paris. The beds, I was told, were in such bad shape that I could have them.

"When a hotel is finished with a bed," the director of house-keeping said to me, "it probably sags; this is no great gift."

I borrowed a queen-sized *tête-de-lit* (headboard) for my bed (which I had yet to purchase), a desk, two minibar cabinets sans minibar, a pair of end tables that even matched the *tête-de-lit,* a cast-iron bistro table stand (no top) and a *porte-bagage*—the wooden rack found in a hotel room where you place your suitcase so you can open it and get into it without breaking your back. I had everything I needed except a dining room table set and a bed for myself. At least I could move out of the kitchen.

13

Beds are sold in France in several parts: the mattress, the box spring and the legs. The word for box spring is *sommier,* which I could never remember, so I went to stores and asked for the *sommelier,* the wine steward.

In one day I think I must have lain down on every real bed in every department store in Paris. (This was exhausting.) I mulled over prices and brand names, fabrics and bedsprings. I endured serious discussions about delivery. The quickest I could have a bed was one week; most beds would take three to six weeks to order.

I didn't have that kind of time. I didn't know if there was a French version of "dial 1-800-MATTRES and leave off the last S for savings." I needed a bed. At BHV they told me if I bought a bed that day, I could have delivery in three days. I played out my own version of the Three Bears. Who's been sleeping in *my* bed?

In the end, when none of the beds I liked and could afford were in stock, I finally asked for a list of the beds that could be delivered immediately and picked the one I could best afford that was the least offensive. I felt like the Princess and the Pea, Mama Bear, Papa Bear and Baby Bear all rolled into one. To this day, it's my dream to replace that mattress.

After I picked the bed, I was asked to pick the legs—a different transaction in a different part of the store with a different cash register. Legs cost twenty-five dollars each; the price depended on their height, bulk and design features. I didn't see how I could get away with fewer than four legs.

14

I decided to head to Lille to buy bed linens. Lille is the Pittsburgh of France: a northern, industrial city that always gets a laugh—or a groan—when you mention it. I first went there years ago on behalf of Born to Shop because it's where most of the French bed linen factory outlets are located. Inquiring minds wanted to know. Now that I had moved to France, I wanted to stock up on overstock. Have beds, will travel for linen.

While Lille has a dull reputation, nothing could be more wrong or out of date. In recent years, the changes in the city have begun to catch up with the image and more and more people go there as tourists. It is the turnaround city for the Eurostar train (Chunnel) so the British visit there in droves and most of the local French people speak English.

The city is also only thirty miles from the Belgian border and one hour's drive from Brussels. It has its own style of cuisine, there's great beer, the architecture is somewhat Flemish and ornate, there's the most famous annual flea market in all of France (dating back to medieval times and always held the first weekend in September), and the second largest art museum in France after the Louvre. Oh yes, did I mention the zillions upon zillions of factory outlets, selling everything, but specializing in bed linens? Yes, I think I did.

After one look at the cost of things in Parisian department stores ($60 to $100 for a designer bed sheet—that's for one sheet not a set), I decided to pop on the train and head to Lille and the factory outlets. I had not brought sheets from the United States because I knew that French bed sizes are different from U.S. bed sizes, so I was willing to travel to get a price break. Besides, I can think of worse ways to spend my time than visiting one of my favorite French cities and going to a bunch of outlet stores.

Lille is not very close to Paris (it's about a five-hour drive, even when speeding along a French highway), but with the Thalys high-speed train, you can be there in one hour. If you do the outlets, the best thing to do is rent a car, as the best ones are out of town—sometimes in suburbs, sometimes in the boonies. I checked into the Hotel Carlton, my regular when I am in Lille because of its location (and good prices). It's also one of the nicest hotels in Lille. Thankfully I had a girlfriend who was living in Lille and she could do the driving, since this industrial city is connected by a maze of highways, cloverleafs and overflies. We rented a Berlingo, a minitruck, and set out straight away for the Porthault (pronounced port-ho) outlet. Judith unfurled a hand-painted sign she made and pasted it to the side of the minitruck: BORN TO SHOP LILLE. We laughed all the way to the highway while I read off my checklist of needs for setting up housekeeping.

Porthault is the most famous brand name in luxury bedding in France and possibly the world. The sheets retail for about one thousand dollars each, depending on size, fabric and the amount of work involved. While traditionally the firm has been known for a very specific kind of print—florals on a bright white background—they have also modernized the line to include embroidered borders, jacquard solids and all sorts of extension products from bathrobes to children's needs. There is also a hotel line and an industrial line.

The Hotel Plaza Athénée in Paris is famous for its custom-made Porthault tablecloths—red geraniums splashed on a white background—which are placed on the tables in the courtyard each May 15 at a party to celebrate the arrival of fine weather and fine linens. Most of the world's top hotels have Porthault terrycloth robes. The Porthault factory outlet sells both the commercial lines as well as the consumer lines; both are deluxe brands released at a small fraction of the regular retail price. A simple one-thousand-dollar sheet costs about one hundred dollars in the outlet store.

The Porthault outlet store is located right within the factory and the factory is so far in the middle of nowhere that locals and even local taxi drivers get lost getting there. (I recently went by taxi—it cost $100 for pick-up at the train station, forty-five minutes waiting time at the outlet and the drive back; this included fifteen minutes of being lost, which I was forced to pay for.) Nonetheless, my girlfriend was by then a pro at finding this outlet and we made it there in a record forty-five-minute drive from downtown Lille.

As in all outlets, the choices were catch as catch can. I didn't find as much as I wanted, but I was able to get two bathrobes for guests ($45 each), a set of matrimonial linens (with deep embroidery, too yummy to pass up at $350 for the whole set and something I told myself I would save for a special event), a plain beige jacquard top sheet ($75) and several of the famous Porthault baby pillows, which I give as gifts. Later in the day I got a beige fitted sheet to match my Porthault top sheet for $9—this helped amortize the expense of a $75 sheet and made me feel like a smart shopper instead of a princess.

We loaded up our truck and returned to town, stopping in Roubaix, perhaps the most famous suburb of Lille, where there are several outlets and two outlet malls, one of which—McArthur Glen Roubaix—is partly owned by Americans and is in the village style most American shoppers are familiar with. The other mall is very French, very ugly, very confusing and tremendous fun. It is named, appropriately enough, L'Usine, which means The Factory. Naturally, I prefer the French one, especially now that I am used to it and have seen enough outlet malls all over France to know there are plenty of outlets that are more American—and attractive—than this one.

I don't mind it when the French adopt some American traits, but I do prefer my outlets to be funky rather than fashionable. It was so crowded at this mall that it took us almost a half hour to find a parking space. That worked up an appetite, so we stopped by the food kiosk and got a waffle with chocolate sauce and a newspaper cone filled with fries, which many locals dip into mayonnaise (yuck). Once we were good and sticky and greasy, we were ready to go shopping.

L'Usine is in a converted warehouse and consists of three floors of shops, some of which offer bargains and some of which sell at regular retail price in the international marketing ploy of It Looks Like an Outlet but It Ain't. There are several brand-name outlets selling famous *marques* (brands) in shoes, clothing, lingerie, sleepwear and, of course, home linens. But Born to Shop research has taught me a system, so my first stop has always been Texaffaires, the Deschamps outlet store, which is a freestanding building next to the warehouse of outlets. There are scads of Texaffaires outlets all over France; there are even a few in easy-to-get-to neighborhoods of Paris—but I like this one because it's a tad raw. That means it feels like a real factory store rather than a fancy boutique passing itself off as a discount source. Merchandise is piled from floor to chest height; tables are laden with towels and sheets and bathrobes; fabric is sold by the meter. Bed linen fabric (called sheeting in the trade) is sold off the bolt—this is extraordinary because it is so wide. In the past, I have bought it to make tablecloths. On that first trip as a Frenchie, I bought duvets and pillows and all sorts of basics that we loaded into the truck before heading into the warehouse building.

It is impossible to do justice to all the stores in the main warehouse. I was just looking for housewares anyway, so I stuck to the jobbers who sell linens and bought a lot of Christian Lacroix, Pierre Frey and Yves Delorme linens at half price.

The next day we went back to Roubaix to the other outlet mall, which was too fancy for my tastes. We then returned to L'Usine so I could buy more Lacroix sheets. After lunch, I hit some of the stores in downtown Lille, which has a large branch of a chain called Eurodif.

Eurodif stores are owned by the same folks who own Bouchara stores (the flagship is next door to Galeries Lafayette in Paris) but they combine the home furnishings branch of the business with the clothing branch in store locations outside of Paris, so they make good one-stop shopping stops for fashion and home style. A trip to Eurodif in Lille was equal to three floors of fun: I bought lamps for the apartment, pot holders, kitchen towels and all sorts of smalls. This taught me one of the sad lessons of Paris shopping: Paris is great for fashion and "licking windows" (the French expression for window shopping), but the provinces turned out to be better for real life needs at fair prices.

By this time, I was commuting from the stores to the hotel and filling up suitcase after suitcase. On my final morning, Sunday, we went to the flea market where the prices are so low you feel like giggling in glee. I truly could have furnished my apartment from this flea market, but the trucking would have been more expensive than the price of the goods. I settled for a few things that I could pack or carry and then somehow get on the train to head back home, home to Paris.

15

I had arrived in Paris with a fistful of names and phone numbers; exactly as when I had moved to New York when I was twenty-one years old. Before, my little list of names had been collected at the beauty parlor by my mother. This time everyone I knew in the States, including mere acquaintances, had friends in Paris that I just had to call. The Gilbert and Sullivan song "I've Got a Little List" kept going through my brain. I had more than a little list; it seemed like an endless list of people I just "had to meet."

Most prominent on the list was a woman named Claire Tuttle, an American who grew up in Connecticut, whose brother Phil was the best friend of Mike's life insurance man. She e-mailed me before I even left the States and invited me to dinner. She sent several e-mails of encouragement. By complete coincidence, the Tuttles lived in the same arrondissement as I did and there was a bus (number 31) that went almost directly from my house to theirs. Still, I got lost on the way, punched their phone number into my French portable phone and got a teenage girl with a perky voice, filled with laughter. The neighborhood I had wandered into wasn't too savory, but she calmed me, gave me instructions and was the nicest teenager I had spoken to in years.

The Tuttles' neighborhood was like a souk of international fast-food eateries, markets and bargain basement shops with people of all colors bustling about on their way home from work, creating a special buzz. I was sure this was the kind of area that never slept. By the time I reached their home, I was already in love with the Tuttles. The address I was given was a small building on a side street, the same size as a New York brownstone, but with gorgeous turn-of-the-century *ciment* tiles on the floor and a curving staircase with the kind of patina that only comes from a hundred years of use. It was a yummy dump, shabby chic with heart.

I walked up to the top floor (six flights, since the first floor is one up in a French building) and breathlessly entered the kind of apartment where you don't even want to talk to your hosts, you just want to catch your breath and look at everything—the stacks of books and records and the overflowing bookcases and shelves made it clear that this was a family that cared more about music and literature than fashion or style. Their furniture didn't match and some of it need reupholstering, but each piece looked like it was from a museum or had been passed down in the family for generations. Blooming orchids filled the fireplace.

The four members of the Tuttle family gathered around me for introductions: Solange, sixteen; Jean-Philippe, fourteen; Claire, who had just arrived from work; and Ty, her husband, who worked at home as a journalist and translator and who sang with the Paris Orchestra. They hardly looked like a typical French family—both Claire and her husband had a distinct New

England WASP, preppy look to them, and a distant air that whispered that their ancestors must have stepped off the *Mayflower* rather than the *Normandie*. As it turned out, part of Ty's family did come to America on the *Mayflower,* whereas Claire was what the French call a half and half: one parent French and the other American. She grew up in Greenwich, Connecticut, summered in France and then moved to France full-time when she was twenty-one. She is a French citizen. She votes left.

Claire was sort of the earth-mother type—calm, organized, in control, with rocklike strength but also nourishing with warmth and support. She was not demanding, but full of listening and laughing: the kind of woman who might have walked across America behind a covered wagon and then cooked a gourmet meal over the campfire before she fought off the Indians. I was put into the rocking chair in the kitchen, while everyone else sat around the kitchen table. As Claire prepared dinner, we all chatted and I told the saga of finding my apartment, the various events that I found suspicious (I was still miffed about having to pay rent as of February 15 when I hadn't even seen the apartment then) and the hardships of my two weeks of living in France.

"I don't know if I am having a hard time because I am newly widowed or living in France is simply harder than I expected," I told the group.

"Not to belittle your grief in any way," Claire said, "but living in France is harder than people coming from the States think. We're all here because we think it's worth it, but don't underestimate the stress of a move like this."

Like proper French citizens, we sat at the table well into the night, sipped a little wine and discussed what the hardships of a move to Paris were and whom they most affected. We decided, like good French socialists might, that many of the obstacles could be overcome with time, patience and money. Indeed, my transition into daily life would have been more seamless if:

- I stayed in a hotel until my apartment was finished—or at least was painted and had beds. I would not have been so frustrated with how hard it was to get a bed or the miserable quality of the bed I bought because I was forced to buy something in stock.
- I knew I was staying in Paris for a longer period of time than a year. Then I would not have been in such a hurry to make things happen, to get settled so I could enjoy the year. It takes at least a year to set up an apartment or a home. Maybe I should have rented a furnished flat for a year.
- I had hired an English-speaking French personal assistant or secretary who could guide me through the dark waters of change. I would have avoided the Twilight Zone feeling that went with not speaking the language very well and not knowing the laws or how to fight back within the system. While friends were helpful, a newcomer really needs a full-time advocate to teach her the ropes and do the dirty work.

We decided after even more wine that when a former tourist chooses to stay for a year, he or she thinks this is a long period of time. But when it comes to setting up housekeeping, getting settled, making friends and learning a city, a year goes by very quickly. It's surely possible to know if you want to stay in Paris after living there for a few months, but it's not possible to put the whole experience into the space of a year.

With a little more wine we concluded that the expat experience in Paris was very much related to the pocketbook, the ability to absorb cultural difference quickly and a strong list of social connections, especially French ones, because the Napoleonic system may theoretically protect little people, but the old-fashioned, good-old-Frog network knew how to get things done behind the rules and paperwork. Money might not buy happiness, but it could buy ease.

16

Not every social outing was as successful as the visit with the Tuttles. There were plenty of lunches and dinners with people who were lovely; I just didn't have anything in common with them. As one woman I know said, "Just because a person speaks English doesn't make him or her your new best friend."

A fair number of the people I began to see often were people I knew from years ago and had lost touch with. My best friend when I was fifteen, Sherry Newman, eventually married a Frenchman and moved to Paris. We reconnected after all those years. A woman I had met in New York in 1969 named Abby married an American businessman in Paris and arrived within the same month I did. I hadn't seen her in thirty years, but it didn't matter.

Mike and I had made friends with a French couple (Marie-Jo and Gerard) with whom we had exchanged houses in 1984. We had stayed in touch with them, but they surely never expected me to be their neighbor. I knew hoteliers and PR people and a few fashion people and retailers and lots of journalists. I was

glad to have so many different contacts and people to call because I did not want to end up in one tiny social group. I was
wary of ending up in a world of only expats or of cliques.

Through twenty years of research on Born to Shop and many
visits with the same group of friends there, I have observed the
social scene in Hong Kong. As much as I love to visit Honkers,
my world there is a closed set. The people who live there full-
time are bored with each other and starving for new blood.
They live in a high-rise fishbowl. I didn't want my entire French
social life tied up in gossip surrounding the same old faces.

I refused to join any of the clubs or women's groups that were
so popular in Paris. There's something called The American Club,
which is actually a cultural group that has many interesting lectures and events. There was AARO, something to do with Americans living abroad. Then there's an alphabet soup of organizations
for wives of ambassadors, wives of transferred businessmen,
wives of the sons of the daughters of the republic, etcetera. These
groups seemed to be organized for the purpose of protecting expats from the real world of France. I moved to France to enjoy the
French and therefore did not join any American groups.

I made certain to devote myself partly to my French friends
and to my hotelier friends, who formed their own international
band, interconnected by the fact that hotel people are like circus
people: they move around a lot. There was also a group of media
journalists based in Paris. This group overlapped with the literary gang, as there are several well-known American authors and
editors who lived in Paris either full-time or part-time. They
gave the best dinner parties because the conversation was lively
and the mix always involved people with good gossip and bad

hair. This gang was as likely to talk about politics, religion and ballet as the use of Rogaine on pubic hair, the newest bistro down the street or the color purple.

Americans are pretty open to newcomers. The French are not. As a result, there are some public-relations women and a few low-in-cash countesses or aristos who can be hired to get you into assorted social circles in Paris. To get into French society takes time and some serious connections. Money helps; a title or some claim to fame is a very nice touch. The ability to speak lyrical French is a plus as well.

Some women go the diplomatic route—there is a large circle of ambassadors' wives who do lunch and cultural events together. There is also a charity circuit in Paris, much of it is dominated by American money or American women who have friends with money who are willing to save French cultural icons. This social avenue is open to those with the price of admission and the right designer dress.

I did not know any out-of-work members of the aristocracy nor have the funds for the charity events but studiously followed up on all my possibilities. I worked very hard at getting out in those early months. I often had to force myself to one more party or one more dinner, when all I really wanted was to stay home and watch TV. I went out only because I heard the memory of my mother's voice ringing in my brain, an echo from when I was twenty-two years old: "No one ever met anyone while sitting at home reading a book."

17

Day-to-day life went rather smoothly, but I was consistently stumped by a new language obstacle or a mechanical problem in my household. The concierge did not seem delighted to help me, even though I put cash in her pocket every time I called her upstairs.

Despite the fact that I had learned the politically correct term of *gardienne,* I still wanted the concierge for my new building to be from central casting, in looks and in spirit. I wanted her to adopt me, take me to her ample bosom (is a French bosom worth having if it isn't ample?) and teach me the secrets of being French, of running a French household. I hoped my concierge would be part of my coaching staff.

She would be almost as wide as she was tall, with wiry gray hair mixed with strands still black and crisp—all of this hair would be pulled back from her face with a hair clip, left to tumble down and then out in a mass of unkept frizz. Her face would be lined but dignified; her nose would be the map of France. Her skin would be blustery, red-veined and chapped, her knuckles gnarly as they held a willow-tipped broom to sweep clean our courtyard. In summer she would use one of those old switches to beat the dust out of carpets hanging on the iron gates and basking in the sunshine. Her cigarette would dangle magically from her lipstick-stained lips, even when she spoke. Her gravelly voice would spit out rapid but perfect French. In fact, any casting call for the chorus for the musical *Les Mis* would find her in a jiffy.

But the real concierges of France have changed. Most of them aren't even French; their French is often not much better than mine. This is a job nowadays occupied more and more frequently by immigrant women. A lot of them are from Vietnam, but there are many from European nations, especially those that were at one time considered third world countries and are now about to be admitted to the European Union.

The concierge of my building came from Slovenia. There was nothing romantic about her or her French accent. She was sort of butch looking in that too-many-potatoes-in-the-pot Eastern European fashion; her French was harsh and gutteral. She had bleached-out hair and big glasses worn on a chain around her neck. She wore no makeup, just a heavy slash of dark red lipstick across her face. In fact, she reminded me of a prison guard I saw in a World War II movie once. She was probably my age, maybe even younger, but there wasn't much feeling of commiseration. She was called simply "madame." She constantly asked me when my French would improve. She *clucked* at me or barked orders, often demanding that I do things that I thought fell under her job description—but everyone needs someone to bully, and I was the new kid on the block, trying to find my way as a stranger in a strange land.

She asked me not to groom my geraniums because the petals fell to the courtyard and then she had to sweep them up. I was in fact the only tenant with flowering plants on the *balcon* and I wondered if she had forced the others into compliance with her wishes. She ruled the building as if it were Stalag 17 and we were the cast of prisoners from the TV show *Hogan's Heroes*.

I was told by my advisory committee of friends who helped me get started and set up in Paris that the way to the concierge's heart was through her wallet. Accordingly, I was very generous, not only with cash tips but with gifts from each of my trips out of town. I even gave her a pair of Porthault pillowcases when I returned from Lille, knowing that such a statusy item would be highly prized by a Frenchwoman. She did not know what they were, nor did she seem to care. I brought her sunglasses with lenses made in the shape of the state of Texas, to explain to her where I was from. She asked if I knew George Bush. I thought about baking her an American lemon cake, but I didn't know how to use the oven.

18

I quickly found myself stuck, trapped, stranded in household tasks. I was, as the French say, *nulle* (stupid) when it came to the workings of even the most basic things in a French apartment. Madame I can-adapt-to-anything did not know how to change a lightbulb in France.

I am not as stupid as I sound. There were three things going against me:

- I did not know there were two different kinds of lightbulbs in France.
- I had never dealt with ceilings that were so high that a stepladder didn't solve the problem.
- For the last twenty-five years of my life, a man had performed the honeydew tasks in the household (Honey do this, honey do that). I actually hadn't changed a lightbulb in more than twenty years.

⨖

Pascale-Agnès called me daily to see how I was doing, and soon realized she would have to teach me the secrets of survival. After hearing my tale about the lightbulb, she came to Paris from her home in eastern France and stayed with me for a weekend to help me get ready for my son, Aaron's, arrival. She taught me a few more tricks to daily living, such as:

- How to divert water to reach either the washing machine or the dishwasher (turn either the L switch or the V switch under the faucet; L equals washing machine, V equals dishwasher);
- How to set the agitation in the washing machine for different types of wash loads, which I discovered is terrifyingly important if you don't want towels to be wringing wet at the end of the cycle;
- How to open the drum of the damn washing machine (press down on both halves of the top);
- Where to dispose of the milk and cereal mush in the bottom of my breakfast bowl or any other mushy leftovers (toilet; the sink drain had a recessed trap);
- Where to store fresh bread (oven);
- How to change a lightbulb (buy fourteen-foot ladder);
- Why the duvet cover has a tail (to tuck it under the mattress so it doesn't move around when you do);
- How to clean the stains in the bathtub (Coca-Cola);
- Why it was important to decalk appliances and put salt into the dishwasher (very hard water in Paris);
- Why the sewing machine didn't work (someone stole

one of the key parts from the box; never should have
bought a product with a box taped back together);

- Why the telephone didn't work (it's French, buy
German brands whenever possible);
- Where to recycle wine bottles (in those large, bright
green igloolike huts all over Paris);
- And how to use a French lamp shade, since they are all
built with a reverse harp, secured by screwing the
lightbulb into the socket *after* the lamp shade is
mounted around the socket.

While Pascale-Agnès has always been somewhat mechanical
and certainly better at building things and working machinery
than I am, she was not a teenage boy. Having already raised a
son, I knew that today's young men have an electronic-digital
gift that must be attached to their thumbs from playing so many
Nintendo games as youngsters. Jean-Philippe Tuttle fit the bill;
he knew everything there was to know about the workings of
telephones, mobile phones, televisions, computers and more.
For the price of six euros an hour, he made house calls.

Directions for installation of major appliances come in fancy
booklets printed in many languages, but small items, such as
telephones and answering machines, have instructions only in
French. My French is fine for asking the price of an item in the
market, but not good enough to read complicated directions, so
Jean-Philippe installed my answering machine, my fax machine,
my computer and my VCR. Anyone contemplating a move to
Paris should insist that among their local contacts there is a
young man who hires out. Jean-Philippe also does dishes and
serves at dinner parties.

19

Before I moved here, I had been to the seventeenth exactly once in my life. I remember it clearly because I was with my husband, it was my birthday and we went to the annual flea market at the Parc Monceau right near my current apartment. I looked up at the stately buildings, the gilt gates of the *parc*, sniffed the expensive air of the real estate and grandly said to my husband, "I would hate to live here, the residents are all so rich they look alike."

I never returned to this area, mostly because there weren't enough stores to make it part of a Born to Shop book. So when I moved there, the only thing I knew about the area was that Monoprix would be my best friend. Monoprix was created in the 1930s after a member of the family that owned Galeries Lafayette went to the United States and saw American dime stores like Woolworth and Newberry. Despite the fact that five-and-dime stores have died out in America, Monoprix has not only thrived in France but is, in my professional opinion (as the Shopping Goddess), one of the best stores in France. Most Monoprix stores consist of two parts: a supermarket and a dry goods store that sells all the basics you might need in real life, including clothes and underwear.

It was the sight of a Monoprix near the place Pereire that made me agree to rent my apartment, but beyond that I had no idea what was in my neighborhood or which of the choices to try first. One of the benefits of living in an area of rich people is that there are excellent restaurants, which I slowly began to test. By chance, one of the up and coming modern bistros of

Paris—A&M Marree—was receiving a lot of press and turned out to be next door to my apartment. With its cozy front room and vaulted back room where the ceiling is created from wine bottles, A&M has a fixed-price menu and a neighborhood feel without being down-market or filled with kids on Rollerblades. Superchefs Guy Savoy and Michel Rostand have their main restaurants in the area; they have also opened a few less expensive, no Michelin stars but great eats eateries just down the street from me. In short, *par hasard* (by accident), I chose one of the best neighborhoods in Paris for foodies.

For services, I ended up making choices based on location (I picked the cleaner across from Monoprix rather than the one in the other direction) or aesthetics—I chose my hairdresser simply because of all the hairdressers in the neighborhood (and there were plenty of choices), I liked what her shop looked like best. I also turned out to like my hairdresser, which was just blind luck. (Christine Boulben, avenue Villiers, 17e.)

As I became a regular, and she got used to my bad French, we began to chat more and more and sort of became friends. I got a free cream rinse every now and then (a four-euro savings). We kissed on each cheek to say hello and goodbye. One day she asked me if I was married.

"Je suis veuve," I told her. I am a widow.

"Merde," she said. Shit.

Of all the things ever said to me when my husband became ill or died, that was the single best response . . . and all anyone really ever had to say.

20

I wanted to cook Aaron's favorite American chocolate cake for his arrival in Paris, not only to welcome him, but to define the apartment as our home. I stood in the kitchen with the cake mix, two eggs and a mixing bowl laid out on the counter. Beyond that, I had no idea what to do. The oven was so complicated to use that at first I thought it was broken; Herr Strumpf had to come over to teach me how to turn it on. Now that I was ready to bake, I discovered I had neither an American measuring cup nor a conversion chart with me.

I had some small experience in a French kitchen from the time we exchanged houses with Marie-Jo and Gerard in Le Mans some twenty years before. That kitchen was almost normal compared to my new kitchen in Paris. The oven in Le Mans had a numbering system from one to eight, that is common in French gas ovens (which actually begin at one-half). My fancy German oven did not have this system, but instead had temperatures in Celsius, yet strangely it only went to 200 C when most ovens went to 230 C or 240 C. Lacking any kind of conversion chart, and not knowing the CNN weather trick (to change Celsius to Fahrenheit, double the temperature then add thirty), I called the office of one of my chef friends.

Chef was not there, so I was passed to the pastry chef, who over the phone taught me how to use my oven. It seemed this great wonder in my kitchen was a very fancy convection oven that took a lot of practice to use properly and worked on a unique heating system. With a few directions from him, I was ready to start cooking. I made Aaron's cake and then, to thank the chef, I baked him some brownies from an American mix. After all, I wasn't about to attempt a French treat for a world famous pastry chef, was I?

21

I began to analyze everything else in the apartment, dragging furniture from one room to another, using felt pads under the legs so that I could slide large pieces across the parquet. I got this idea from having visited the great museums of the Soviet Union back in the dark ages of tourism when the Evil Empire made everyone wear felt slippers. The care and feeding of ancient buildings was not anything I knew about from my life in a ranch house in San Antonio, Texas, or a builder's colonial in Westport, Connecticut. I found myself turning to textbooks and history books to learn more about the lifestyle at the turn of the nineteenth century so that I could better understand how to clean my apartment. My homes in the United States never had thirteen-foot ceilings. While Belle Époque Madame living in a flat as grand as mine was not expected to dust, someone had to do it. How did she reach? (Answer: extension poles.)

As I saw it, these historical points of reference also dictated the interior decoration. I had chosen a different color palette in Paris from what we had in Westport, but stayed with the same look so that Aaron would feel at home. I flirted with several dif-

ferent style ideas, from the brashly modern and slightly *fou*
Philippe Starck pieces, which could be mixed with bright colors
like purple, red and orange to the arts and craftsy brights of
Englishwoman Tricia Guild. I even liked the idea of mixing
Starck with kitsch, as I have always had a terrible weakness for
kitsch—and it was readily available in Paris.

I thought of the scads of hotel rooms I had adored over the
years, places where I had found comfort in bed with any number
of Louis's, with draped beds that were, for some reason I never
understood, called *lits à la polonaise* (Polish beds). But formal ain't
moi, so I fell right into my same old habit of mixing and matching a
few good pieces with lots of junk. As I surveyed the living room,
the biggest laugh was the china cabinet—a glass and wood affair
with the look of having been left in the barn over the past one
hundred years. You would never doubt it was old and came from a
flea market at a good price. The truth was, it came from Galeries
Lafayette, was the most expensive single item in the apartment
(even with my tourist discount card, which yes, you can use on
furniture) and was purchased because it was stunning and exactly
fit the space. Besides, I needed the storage offered by this cabinet.

I figured out that within the first three weeks of living in that
apartment, I had spent almost $10,000 to get the living room
and dining area going. And this doesn't include dishes, cutlery
or table linen.

Item	Cost	Source
Sofabed	$1,000	Galeries Lafayette
Dining room table	$1,000	Cedre Rouge
Green velvet armchairs (two)	$ 400	Flea market, Vanves
Dining chairs (six/disaster)	$ 250	Flea market, Vanves

Item	Cost	Source
New dining chairs (six)	$ 650	Flea market, Chatou
Serving cart	$ 150	Flea market, Vanves
Étagère	$1,800	Galeries Lafayette
Living room lamps (two)	$1,200	BHV
Side tables (two)	$ 350	Habitat

I started off with one set of dishes, but soon had three—one set for the kitchen (for Aaron and his guests, since I was afraid they would break the good dishes), one set for dress-up (obviously too good to ever use) and one more set that I was building as a creative notion of mixed pieces and performance art. This was to be a set of dishes from all the restaurants I visited during the year, sort of an advanced game of stolen ashtrays. Since I was not clever enough to figure out how to steal an entire dinner service, I just asked the chef for it. I kept a waterproof marker in my handbag so the chef could autograph the back of the piece.

22

I had learned to play the Chef Game before I moved to France. My friend Alec, an American in Paris with an observant eye for cross-cultural nuances, made the perfect comment on the Chef Game and why it is so important in France.

"They don't have baseball teams in France," he said, "so they have to root for the chef."

This sport means keeping track of dozens of chefs—new chefs; chefs trained with the famous chefs; chefs who move to new venues or open up new bistros; chefs in hotels; chefs who give up the rat race and downsize. The new Michelin guide comes out every March; its much anticipated release brings rounds of intellectual discussion and a hurried need to get into restaurants that must be tried immediately. To admit you cannot gain a reservation is embarrassing; to admit you don't know who is being discussed is the kiss of death at any dinner party.

Besides the Michelin Red Guides, there is another good rating system—Gault Millaut (say go me-yo), but for some reason the GM announcements and assessments do not usually make news as the Michelin ones do. The Zagat guide arrived in Paris the same year I did and strangely enough, immediately became the second most important judge of restaurants and true-rue table talk.

Published in both French- and English-language editions, the Zagat guide used the same format it uses in the United States, but took opinions only from French locals. Zagat named Taillevant the number one restaurant in Paris that year, a fact that was debated across cafés and dinner tables for months. Obviously, if you hadn't been to Taillevant at least once, you couldn't play the game. In fact, it took a bit of a financial investment to get into this team sport and it wasn't for everyone. Because my funds were limited, I used my lists of must-trys on visitors from out of town who wanted to take me out to dinner and socialized with those who played the antichef game: where to find great eats at fixed-price restaurants for fifteen to thirty euros.

23

In the rustle of party clothes that accompanied my early weeks in Paris, I was invited to several dinner parties given in my honor to help get me started. The invitations came in different ways, which made it seem all the more exciting: one woman said she was having a dinner party anyway and I must join them and be the guest of honor. Oh? Okay.

This turned out to be a very dressy thing for twelve at an oval ebony table in a formal dining room hung with Impressionist paintings and mirrors. Dinner was served by a staff of three. Everyone spoke English, although the group was international and not all American expat. The dress code was little black dress with extravagantly fringed rich-hippie shawls and big earrings.

The party that was more clearly in my honor was arranged before I left Westport and was given by a woman I had never even met, an author who liked my work and wanted to welcome me and help me meet new friends. Her apartment was also very fancy, but her style was funky. The dress was hip; the guests were varied. They were intellectuals. There was a heap of unmatched dishes collected from flea markets piled up on the buffet; three tables were set in three different rooms in the house; the host and hostess rotated tables. There was only one in help, a borrowed butler.

As I shyly stood by listening to one conversation, I tried to keep a straight face when I heard two women discussing the triumph of the hostess's new paint job in the dining room.

"Would you call this color lime?" one woman asked the other.

"Oh no, my dear! Lime is Versailles. This is kiwi!"

The most glamorous party was given at the Hotel Meurice. I had just arrived, a hotelier friend was my houseguest. We were invited to dinner in the main dining room, one of the fanciest rooms in Paris, where eight of us sat at a round table and laughed all night. I had never met most of the other guests, but there we were, living in Paris, dining at a one-star table, sipping the best wines in France and wondering how the time fled so quickly.

The waiters were patiently setting the tables for breakfast when we realized that it was one A.M. and time to quit. It was one of those evenings when everyone not only swapped cards and swore to get together again, but actually did. I cried when I got home at two A.M., possibly from exhaustion but also in a wistful state of frustration, so sad that Mike wasn't there. He would have loved that dinner party. It seemed such a cruel joke that I was having the time of my life and he was dead.

24

I first thought that the dinner parties in my honor were unusual. Hey, I just came to town, *merci* for the fete. I'm flattered and grateful, ya'll.

I soon learned that my arrival was just an excuse for a dinner party. I was merely the flavor of the month. The people I connected with in Paris were always giving dinner parties. Out-of-town visitors to Paris wanted to take me to the latest restaurants, but locals invited me into their homes. Except for my friends Paul and Abby, who hold a regular dinner party at the

Chinese restaurant Davé each Sunday night, there were few in-vitations to restaurants from locals.

These down-home dinner parties were often held even on "school nights" (during the week) with people sitting down to table around nine P.M.——not leaving until after midnight. Even if guests were invited for eight P.M., few showed up much be-fore nine P.M., which meant I had either eaten all the snacks and some of the napkins before we got to table, or was starving and dared not drink too much for fear of becoming silly . . . or throwing up. In time, I learned to eat a light meal around six-thirty P.M. before I got ready for the evening.

Unless the hostess has specified otherwise, the dress was al-ways dinner-party chic for women. Men usually arrived from the office and were allowed to take off their ties, or at least to loosen them. Women also arrived in their office attire or, when able to change their clothes, usually wore something that fell in the chic but not too-too area. I found this a fashion territory filled with land mines. Frenchwomen wore a lot of suits; either matched suits or country-looking suits, with pieces that some-times wouldn't appear to match to anyone except another Frenchwoman. Many American women opted for black, which I don't wear very often and save for out-of-town travel.

I relied on the rich-hippie look——lots of velvet, layers, tex-tures, colors, scarves, beads, camellias and bangles teamed with designer earrings, a bow in my hair, mules (usually worn with socks) and a fresh manicure. My manicured, lengthy silk-wrapped nails reinforced to Frenchwomen that I was indeed American. In Paris, American women are known by their nails.

Indeed, there was a Berlin Wall of silence dividing what a Frenchwoman would wear and what an American one wore. It took a hell of a lot of study for an American woman to pull off the French thing. Usually it was easier to just grasp what was right and what was wrong in each social group.

Vintage clothing was appreciated in this crowd; you did not need designer labels if your presentation was creative or original. It was always better to dress up than to dress down when visiting a French home. On the other hand, no Frenchwoman short of Marisa Berenson or LuLu de la Falaise would be caught dead in anything that wasn't boring. Frenchwomen admired style on others, but usually went for safe style when it came to dressing themselves.

As for Frenchmen and their sense of fashion, well, what can you say about a group of the population that wears short-sleeve shirts with ties (in summer) and is issued an ocher–olive green plaid sports jacket at birth and never takes it off until hospice care?

You knew it was going to be a good dinner party only if the men were all dressed in black. If their black shirts were open to the waist they were gay, but it was going to be a great night.

No matter how well you knew the host and hostess in Paris, you dared not arrive without a gift. Although cultural guides to survival in France tell you it is rude to bring flowers or wine, these were still the most common gifts at the parties I went to. I tried to be more original and brought items from America that were either newly launched products unknown in France or foodstuffs that were hard to find in Paris, such as Philadelphia cream cheese. I once brought a boxed Dryel dry cleaning kit, before it was introduced in France. (Big success; thankfully the recipient had a clothes dryer—which I did not know was not that common.)

I divided the day of each dinner party between homework

and nap time, since I am by nature a lark and like to go to sleep at ten P.M. Any evening out in Paris demanded at least a two-hour nap. Homework consisted of reading newspapers in French and English. Then I would go online and read the *New York Times*. I learned that sex, politics and religion—the exact topics we have been taught to avoid in the United States—were the precise subjects everyone wanted to talk about in Paris. While Americans have a talk-show mentality, talking a lot about themselves and saying very little, the French, and the Americans who live in Paris, prefer to talk about real issues and not personal matters.

25

My son, Aaron, had been to Paris many, many times since his birth, first to visit his aunt Judy and then to accompany me on Born to Shop research trips during his February school vacation. He used to groan and ask me why we couldn't go to Florida like normal people. He did not suffer in silence and made it clear—year after year—that being in France may have been my idea of heaven but was not his.

Now that his father had died and I was spending a year in Paris, it was important to me that he not resent my choice. Even in this experimental year abroad, I was torn between wondering if I should have stayed at home and suffered in silence until he was finished with college . . . or if I had a right to place my own mental health first. Motherhood, thy name is guilt.

If my son had loved Paris before I moved there or even had his own fantasies about life in France, it would have been easier for me. If he'd been an exchange student or enjoyed speaking French, it certainly would have helped. If we had made the decision about my move together, it probably also would have been easier. I felt that I had deserted him, especially in his time of need. Was I selfish? Did he understand my point of view? Did a child ever think of a parent's well-being?

There is a scene in the first episode of the television show *Six Feet Under* in which the widowed mother announces to her sons that they are grown and she is moving to Florida. One son is shocked, the other says "hey, great." I thought about that a lot because it seemed to me that moving to Florida was socially acceptable, but moving to Paris was not.

Aaron brought with him two friends, one girl and one guy. If he was the accidental tourist, they were not. They were clearly in it for the free place to sleep in Paris. The young man had never been to Paris and was a bundle of nervous energy from the minute he walked into the apartment and asked how to flush the toilet. The girl had seen it all and done it all; she went directly to the telephone to call her friends in Paris and Brussels. She had her own international phone card. She spoke French perfectly.

The apartment was suddenly vibrating with not only the energy of three extra people, but from music created by Aaron and his friend Rich. The girl was adorable, but it was clear to me that she was not in love with my son. She liked to eat and already knew how to play the Chef Game, so she was good enough company at my table.

The apartment was far from finished when they arrived, but there was space enough for everyone and I perked up with that feeling a mom always gets when her baby (even if he towers over her) comes home and when a house is suddenly filled with people. I went instantly from living alone in Paris to being a mommy hen with three chicks. I cooked and cleaned all the time—things I don't normally like to do that much—and enjoyed every second of it. Life bubbled over.

We went to markets and shopped. A large portion of every day was spent showing off My Paris, a not-so-subtle attempt to convince Aaron that Paris wasn't such a bad spot after all. We ate many dinners at home so that I was able to test new recipes. I gave casual dinner parties and invited over some of my new French friends, including the Tuttle family. Aaron immediately bonded with the two Tuttle children, which I hoped gave him a feeling of having family in France also. After each dinner, while I did the dishes and prepared dessert, Aaron and Rich gave concerts for the guests.

We also went to concerts. I got tickets to everything I thought the kids would like. Harry Connick Jr was a hit; Brian Ferry was a disaster. I let the kids go to Amsterdam for a day trip so they could smoke a joint legally. I did everything I could to make sure that Aaron had fun, saw the best points about life in Paris and felt comfortable with the idea of living in France. I didn't know if I'd stay a year or a lifetime, but I felt that if Aaron liked Paris, I would have permission to stay . . . and to have a good time.

 *Spring*

Café Royal Pereire, place Pereire, 17e
Pour boire: café au lait

Once Aaron had visited, I felt somewhat settled, as if I had passed the first test of living in Paris. Not "Phew, that's over" but still a rite of passage, a rung up the ladder to the new world. When the kids left, I began going to a new café, one closer to home that they had made their headquarters: the plain vanilla café located on the corner of my street, next to my bank, the news kiosk and the metro station—and just across from Monoprix.

The Royal Pereire is one of those places that becomes part of your life simply because it's there and serves a purpose. There were few gee-whiz charms, just the usual booths, bistro tables, wooden chairs and carte du jour. However, there was also a glass-enclosed patio—with enormous windows that were open in summer—where I sat in the exact same corner every day, writing in my notebook or watching the passing parade of punksters on Rollerblades, mixed-race young lovers, nannies with poussettes *(strollers) and harried mademoiselles with dry cleaning tucked under one arm, market basket on the wrist and cell phone to the ear, pressed against velvet hair band.*

26

It was April in Paris. I was not the only person who wanted to celebrate. A huge number of new products were launched, as if all of France also had spring fever.

I must confess that I have always had a weakness for new products. I traced this passion directly to my mother, who tried everything new ever put on the shelves in the grocery stores of our lives. Because she was a post–World War II bride, my mother was the original participant in the "Plastics" (as it was so hilariously nailed in *The Graduate*'s most memorable line) revolution. I remember the introduction of Saran Wrap, TV dinners, pizza pie (as we called it then) and Dove soap. I have remained fascinated by new products and consider it part of my job to buy them and test them.

Spring in Paris that year was heaven for the consumer—especially for me, since I was not used to the plethora of new products launched each spring and fall as if they were fashion products. I walked through stores almost in a daze, buying and testing, testing and laughing. I bought spray-on foam toothpaste (not a winner) and pantyhose that moisturized my legs (or so it claimed). I bought a pumice stone in stick form for my lips, which needed exfoliating after winter (or so I was told) . . . and then lipstick that would plump them up. I discovered a new hair color application system—the colorant was in a gel stick form and looked just like deodorant. I briefly wondered if it was for the hair under my arms, but realized that more and more French-women shave under their arms these days. *Mais oui.*

There were the usual new fragrance launches, which have always amused me but were not as silly as many of the other spring offerings. Spring, after all, was get-ready-for-bathing-suit season; a raft of diet and slimming products suddenly flooded the stores. The French seem to believe that you can take a pill to cure anything. If the pill won't do the trick, there's always a cream, a spray or a series of glass vials of candy-colored liquid that can either be consumed or rubbed in—or both. There were new treatments for cellulite, bust firming, tanning and promoting your body's ability to tan when the time came. (There was little sun in Paris that April, so everything was in the promise to come.)

The craze for *bien-être*—well-being—had just begun. Spas were opening in hotels; day spas were being launched. The stores were filled with products to use at home to cure an ill or bring yourself more peace, less stress or that all elusive sense of well-being. Everything that couldn't be cured by pill was modified by a treatment. Suddenly shampoos that fixed problem hair came on the market, including my favorite—an anti-aging shampoo that rejuvenated the hair.

It was also a big spring for *sockettes*—minisocks. I have never been able to explain this, but the French seem to be the world's best makers and marketers of, of all things, socks. My husband loved to go shopping in Paris for socks. Walter Wells has admitted to me that he loves the sock department at Galeries Lafayette.

Be they men's or women's socks, there are not only scads to choose from, but there are also new launches and product categories. So it was the spring of the *sockette,* a fancy Ped kind of thing that was worn with high heels in lieu of pantyhose. Truth be told, I wore both—but then, I am, deep inside, American, and will never be French enough or tan enough to go without stockings. The fad, featured in all the fashion magazines, was the kind of thing that was so ugly it was hot. I wore mine with a plain beige, extremely conservative suit and pearls, so my look was boring-boring-boring-wwwwwhaaaat?

The spring season for new products was not limited to clothes and beauty products or items that you would expect to be influenced by the cycles of fashion or *la mode*. There were plenty of new products launched in the grocery store as well, including candy bars in tube shape, Kit Kat bars in balls that looked like moth balls and at least half a dozen different morning cereal products in either bar format or with hefty doses of chocolate. The country that invented the *pain au chocolat* did not see this as enough of a contribution to society, and felt compelled to launch Choco-Smacks.

More interesting were the flower-flavored *sirops* and the carbonated lemonades, which came in glorious colors, but some dubious flavor concepts. I tested *rose, violette* and *mandarine,* but took a pass on *pomme verte* (green apple) and *menthe* (mint). If man were meant to drink green apple lemonade, green apples would grow from lemon trees. Besides, could mint lemonade be anything more than fizzy mouthwash?

27

Trust me on this one: croissants made with sunflower seed oil instead of butter are not as good as you would like them to be.

28

In my many years of Born to Shop researching, I used to think that the chocolate fish for sale in France toward the end of March and in early April, usually during Easter period, were of religious import—something to celebrate Jesus' ability to feed the village with only a few fish. As it turns out, the fish are in honor of April Fish Day, which is April first and corresponds to April Fools' Day. There is only one practical joke in France (it's a small country), so in the old days, paper fish were secretly attached to the rear of some unsuspecting soul (or sole).

So when my old friend Karen Fawcett, the woman who owns the BonjourParis Web site (www.bonjourparis.com), called me and told me to be outside my apartment in fifteen minutes, dressed for messy weather and with my checkbook, I asked if this was an April Fish joke.

"No" she said. "We are driving to Chatou."

I had never heard of Chatou, but it turned out to be a suburb of Paris situated on the Seine and home to a famous fair, held each spring and fall. Officially known as the Chatou Ham Fair, this is a ten-day celebration with hundreds of *brocante* dealers who drive in from all over France and set up a tent village with dirt streets and an entire catering section where pork products are cooked and served. You can get there on the RER train, but Karen had the car so she could do some serious shopping.

Even though it was a weekday, we were dressed in the Parisian early spring weekend uniform—jeans and wax jackets (wax-coated rain gear) with lug-sole shoes. Neither rain nor snow nor sleet nor tourists were going to get between us and the bargains . . . or the pork chops. We parked in an open field, tromped through some mud and arrived at the fair, where my heart missed every other beat for a full five minutes. Chatou, *quelle fête*—where were you when I needed to furnish my apartment in a hurry?

Stretched out before us, in an organized fashion that would have made the commander of a field hospital proud, was an entire city of junk—good junk. The collection was so enormous that it made Vanves look like amateur night at the Grand Old Opry. There were no tourists, although there were dealers. The vendors were friendly; a few tried their half-forgotten high school English on me. Most of them sold a country-rustic look, which is the look I do so that I went drooling from tent to tent and booth to booth. Even the scent of cooking bacon didn't make me drool as much as the endless possibilities sold by these vendors.

I bought a few cheese plates; Karen bought an old tea chest. But I made a mental note that if anyone ever asked me when was the best time to move to Paris and start over, I'd whisper *"Chatou, mon amour, je t'adore."*

29

I have long thought that my birthday should be a national holiday. I love not only my birthday, but the two weeks around it when I receive calls and gifts and luncheon invitations and bask in the glory of the dawning spring season. As my birthday approached a few months after Mike died, I was in a panic: I didn't want to ignore the date because I was afraid I'd sit home and cry and feel sorry for myself. I couldn't afford to give a party at a restaurant for my old and new Paris friends. The apartment was far from ready for any serious entertaining. Being in Paris suddenly didn't seem very special; self-pity was beginning to creep into my mind. Uh-oh.

Superchef Alain Ducasse came to my rescue by reminding me of the pact of our "Club Thirteen," a pledge among a small group of friends whose birthdays fell on the thirteenth day of various months who had agreed to spend birthdays together whenever possible. (His is September 13.) I was invited to lunch at his fanciest Paris restaurant. I asked my friend Philippe from Monoprix and Galeries Lafayette to join me. Although Philippe's birthday was not on the thirteenth of any month, I knew he would enjoy M. Ducasse—one of the most creative men I know. I secretly hoped they could cook up a little business between them. Because of Born to Shop, I knew some interesting people in Paris and I felt it was my job to introduce them to each other.

Philippe, in exchange for this very choice invite, offered to give me a drinks party in the executive offices of Galeries Lafayette, which had never before been opened to the public. He additionally offered champagne and even birthday cake from Dalloyau, one of the most famous pâtisseries in France. When I found out how much it would cost (fifty dollars per cake), I baked a large American birthday cake in my American sheet pan in my German oven, which was then brought to the offices by the store's French chauffeur. I do indeed understand the concepts of both luxe and brand, but when a fifty-dollar cake serves at most eight people, I could not splurge—even with someone else's money. Besides, we had a more global concept going.

The American cake was more amusing to everyone than anything from a French confectioner could ever be; sheet cakes were rare in France. This in itself was an epiphany; I realized that having brought this cake to the party represented my new position in Paris—Shopping Goddess, Style Guru and Mavenesse of Mixed Cultures. No matter how much cultural savvy you gain, a foreigner will never be French, so it was far more fun to mix it all up. The lesson of the birthday cake became one of the foundations to my entertaining tradition in Paris.

About thirty people showed up at the party—we were a half-and-half mix of old friends and soon-to-be friends, all journalists. After cake and champagne, there were words from Philippe and from Karen Fawcett. When I first got to Paris, I organized an electronic magazine of fashion and trend news sponsored by Galeries Lafayette for BonjourParis, so the two of them represented my greatest American-Franco alliance. Both welcomed me officially to Paris and wished me a happy birthday and a *bonne commencement* on my new life . . . and the next fifty-two years. Karen presented me with a BonjourParis T-shirt and Philippe gave me a Galeries Lafayette nylon tote bag. I cut the cake and made a wish.

30

The party ended around eight P.M.; I was the last to leave. I went home alone where I took off my French designer dress, my French makeup, tied my hair out of my face with a French scarf and pulled on my new birthday suit. You see, my birthday is in the middle of April, always near Easter.

When I was a child and everyone in my school class was getting a new Easter dress, my mother allowed me to pick out a new dress too and later a suit, for Passover and my birthday. This is a ritual I still practice each year. But this year, my official birthday suit was a sweat suit from the Bleu Blanc outlet store down the street from my apartment. I was never before a sweats kind of person. I figured if you were putting each leg into trousers anyway, the trousers might as well be jeans or real clothes.

I stood with Jerry Seinfeld on this issue: people who wear sweat suits have given up hope. Yet as spring broke through Parisian rains, leaves turned acid green as they burst onto branches and *hortensias* (hydrangeas) were sold in big pots at flower shops, I felt the need to buy my first sweat suit, to settle into a comfortable skin that was soft and cuddly, that would gave me the hugs I craved that were no longer there for me. Was the worst thing about being a widow the lack of someone to hug you? Could a sweat suit solve this problem?

For my fifty-second birthday, I left the ball alone, went home and happily slipped into my sweat suit. I snuggled into my bed overlooking the flowers on the balcony, ate the last piece of birthday cake with gooey fingers and turned on the TV with the clicker. The programs were in French and I understood little, but it didn't matter. I was moving on.

31

In America, in my old life, I did as little as possible on Sundays. That's why football was invented, right? Life in America seemed all too hectic—too many roles to combine as wife, mother, housekeeper, cook, travel agent and author with a certain amount of income to generate each month. I needed to give myself a day of rest each Sunday.

But Sundays in Paris were a different story. Sundays in Paris were meant for passing a *bon dimanche,* so I had long ago worked out a Sunday routine for Paris:

- I got up early—headed over to the flea market at the Porte de Vanves, the best in Paris.
- When I finished at the flea, I walked back toward the metro on a parallel block where there was a Sunday food market. I always bought my Sunday meal—invariably a roast chicken and some potatoes, maybe fresh radishes and carrots or a cheese and a homemade loaf of bread, preferably *sésame* (pronounced ses-sam).
- Picnic lunch would then be held in my hotel room, with possibly a little help from the minibar, but usually I had already stocked the room with my own stash of drinks, so I saved on minibar prices.
- After lunch, before I lived in Paris, that is, I would take the bus—or walk if it was a nice day—to the Champs Elysées where I bought one or two of the London Sunday papers and then either went to a movie (the most English-language—VO—movies are on the Champs Elysées) or popped into Sephora, always open on Sundays as are most of the stores on the CE, except for my beloved Monoprix.
- After the film, I strolled the CE and stopped for a fast food fix, sometimes at McDo, then returned to my hotel where I had a hot bath, got into bed, read the newspapers and watched TV.

Once I was living in Paris, I needed to change my approach. Sundays were as special as ever, but my needs were different. I began to alternate the schedule a bit because I didn't want to go to the flea market every week. My apartment was quickly looking like a flea market of its own.

Sometimes I worked at my desk in the early hours, then did some cleanup tasks around the apartment before going to rue Poncelet, my neighborhood street market—one of the most famous food markets in Paris. I did the usual Sunday shopping and bought my traditional Sunday chicken and flowers, popped into the grocery stores—which were open on Sunday mornings in that part of Paris—and rolled my little wheely wheeler (the French market basket on wheels) up and down the streets, filled with French bounty.

In the first months, I bought my chickens from the butcher at Poncelet market. By spring, I began to experiment a little—I went next door to the butcher, to a supplier named Divay, one of the more famous names in foie gras in Paris, which also sold chickens and other foodstuffs. Here I bought my chicken, as well as a plastic container filled with stuffed grape leaves and whatever other delectables were in season or whispered my name. The Chicken Man, who stood out in the street in front of the rotisserie, got to know me, called me *"ma petite Américaine"* and gave me the chicken juice in a glass jar. It was not that unusual to get things in glass jars at Paris markets, but usually you were asked to pay extra for the jar or to bring it back next week. The Chicken Man gave me the jar each week as a gift.

The fruit and vegetable man also knew me. I tried all the various vendors before becoming a regular at Fruitée Fruits. At first I thought the vendor was just a friendly guy who was truly delighted to see me. I think he also delighted in cheating me by a few cents, but this is a hazard in any market where nothing is written down . . . and a paranoia of foreigners who fear there is always a small "gringo tax" by way of a few pennies that go astray.

Sometimes I picked a different Sunday street market. The rue des Levis street market wasn't far from my apartment. I would go on the metro and then walk home, my wheely wheeler bouncing along behind me. I found this market didn't have as much soul as Poncelet, so I didn't go very often. The really big adventure was to go over to the Left Bank.

The hardest market for me to get to—because of transportation schemes—was the Raspail Bio Market, the market with the best *rôtis* chickens in Paris. For "Bio" say BO as in "body odor"; this is a rather recent trend in selling foodstuffs in both street markets and grocery stores, the French equivalent of organic. This two-block affair, the most famous of the bio markets in France, was held regularly alongside the Lutetia Hotel on the Left Bank. I began to go there simply as research for *Born to Shop Paris*. Unfortunately, I got hooked.

I say it is unfortunate because I was often tempted to go there by taxi (twelve dollars please) and the chicken that I adored was the most expensive chicken in all of Paris, probably in all of France. And this doesn't include the expenses incurred on the Chicken Stroll, the walk through the market before I even got to my bio chicken vendor. I would have spent twenty dollars on po-tato latkes, which are called *galettes* in French. The Galette Man actually has a reputation all over Paris, especially strong on the Left Bank, where rich Americans don't mind shelling out the, uh, dough for pancakes that can make a dinner party an event. The Galette Man makes his golden treasures right there in the marketplace. You could faint from the scent of grilling onions, cheese and thinly sliced potatoes, which are even better than the latkes my Grandma Jessie used to make. The bad news is that they cost two euros each and just like the potato chip company said, you can't eat just one.

While several vendors sell *poulets rôtis* (rotisserie chickens), the one I fell in love with offered them in three sizes and therefore three prices (this is not that unusual). His chickens were outrageously expensive because they are *fermier* (farm) chickens which is more or less the equivalent of a free-range chicken in the United States. This vendor puts the juice into the chicken bag (I prefer the jar), but ooh-la-la what juice. It is made with diced cucumbers, leeks, herbs and things you don't think you even want to eat but turn out to be aromatic and delish. So delish, in fact, that I don't ruin this chicken by spicing it up with mustard (although I do think it needs a dash of *fleur de sel,* the lumpy French salt).

Sometimes I sat at my place at the kitchen table and tipped my nose into the chicken bag and breathed in the herbal scent. When we first switched over to euros, and the Bio Chicken Man told me that I owed him twenty-two for one chicken, I insisted that he made a mistake in the calculations. At the Poncelet market, where my Chicken Man gives me juice in a jar, I paid eight euros for a great chicken. Cucumber chick from Bio Man was twenty-two. The experiences of the two chickens were totally different, but I cannot afford too many twenty-two-euro chickies.

A perfect Sunday would find me feeling rich enough to splurge on this chicken. I would make the slow trip across town (no number 84 bus on Sundays) with three different metro trains between me and my dream chicken. Then I would buy all I could and return home for chicken, *galettes* and salad for lunch, a videotape in English, a nap and then an afternoon walk.

It was a giant step forward when I decided that I didn't have to be busy every minute, that there was no need for incessant

Born to Shop research; that I would not drown if I sat down to read a book and look at the flowers across the balcony. In fact, I began to finally realize that Sundays meant literally taking the time to stare at the flowers.

32

One of the first things I bought when I moved into my apartment was a television set, which I plugged in and placed on the kitchen floor, next to my beach mat bed nest. The set didn't work immediately, but I noticed a loose white cable on the floor, so I connected that to the set (look out, Mr. Edison) and *voilà,* the TV still didn't work. I went to the local hardware store, where they explained that I needed male and female plugs for the cable. Who knew?

I returned to my kitchen, carefully checked the sex of the plug, got plugged in and this time it did work. I had not only the regular five channels of French TV, but some sort of cable system with an additional twenty-three channels. The Tuttles came over and checked it out after I asked them to explain to me why I received cable TV but had no known subscription.

"Sh," they cautioned. "Don't tell anyone."

They announced that I had some sort of illegal setup that I should enjoy and profit from—gift horses were a rare commodity in France.

There is an entire French subculture that takes pride in cheating the system, that has learned to welcome the odd chance freebie or one-off piece of good luck. For the most part, services in France are expensive, but even public transportation—which is about $1.50 per ride—is subject to the cheat-if-you-can policy. There's even a verb for it, *resquiller*. Some people don't pay bus fares as a matter of principle, although I have yet to figure out what this principle is. It must be that they think life in France is expensive, that they pay a lot of money in taxes and for products and don't get much in return, so they are entitled to a free ride at the system's expense whenever possible. Every now and then there are bus ticket inspections, with fines for those who do not have a properly validated ticket stub or a citywide transportation card.

But if you can get cable television without paying for it, good for you. Just don't brag about it, because someone who pays for his or her cable TV will turn you in to the authorities (*dénoncer*). Contrary to what you may have learned about the French from World War II films, denouncing others is an old sport that goes way back and still continues. For the most part, however, people look the other way because they are not without sin.

So in the privacy of my own kitchen I enjoyed a little piracy, although I mostly watched the main public channels or LCI (say el-say-ee), the French version of CNN. I had no English-speaking channels, which was fine as I desperately needed to improve my French, but it was hard going. I'd say my comprehension level on the news was less than 50 percent. I was just grateful the weather was done with pictograms.

33

One of the best things about living in Paris is that everyone you know comes to town. When people go to New York, they are too busy to call old friends. When people know they are coming to Paris, the first thing they do is send you an e-mail to arrange a get-together. Some come regularly, others come every now and then. A few are first-timers. Some of these people wanted to see my apartment, to know what it was really like to live in Paris. Actually they wanted to see the apartment and know how much I paid in rent so they could decide if they were envious or not. Regardless, they thought that knowing someone who actually lived in Paris made their trip more interesting.

Other visitors wanted me to get them reservations in places they feared they couldn't get into on their own and then invited me to join them so they didn't look like they were taking advantage of me. A few wanted me to take them shopping, or create for them a personal shopping itinerary. There was a small percentage of visiting parents who had college-age kids doing a semester or year abroad. These parents always took me to lunch because they wanted to make sure I'd be there for the kids if there was an emergency.

Most of them just wanted to share their Paris with me, at least for an evening.

Some visitors were one-offers, as I called them—people who were on a one-off visit, just in Paris once in their lives or once every few years. Then there were the regulars. I nicknamed these guys the visiting firemen. They came often and knew what they were doing and where they were going.

The visiting firemen were a huge help in making Paris work for me in the beginning and are still an important reason to live here. As Ernest Hemingway once said, "If you sit long enough at the Café de la Paix, everyone you know will walk by." The modern version of that is sooner or later, everyone you know will send you an e-mail.

Since I wasn't dating anyone, the firemen were the ones who took me to all the new restaurants and old favorites. Together we tried out the changes in *cartes* and chefs, the wines of various vintages and the foods as they came into season. The firemen always seemed to have more money than I did and ordered better wine. They were on holiday, which made my time spent with them like being on holiday too.

The firemen also seemed to have great friends. Sometimes I would have dinner with people I knew who would then say that they were meeting other friends in Paris later in the week and would I join them . . . or that their friends the so-and-so's were coming at a later date and would I mind if they called me. Of all these fix-up friends, only one set turned out to be total duds.

As I look back on many of these social dates, I cannot remember the names of all of the people involved—I just remember what fun we had. Who was that couple from Australia, the vintners who were friends of Alan's? What was the name—first, last, anybody out there?—of that couple from Miami who was making the TV show? And John and Audrey, they were terrific, I remember them fondly—but did they have a last name? Come to think of it, was Audrey's first name Arlene?

They were from L.A., ah yes, I remember it well. He had

fabulous dancing eyes and an easy laugh; she told great shopping stories. God, they were fun. As Maurice Chevalier was quick to point out, we remember more the memory of things than the reality. She wore pink, she wore blue . . . who cares? They were fabulous. And the lamb was good that night too.

34

Mother told me not to talk to strangers, and I did pay attention to everything mother said. But as an adult, well, it's something I have always done. I have been talking to strangers on airplanes for years. When I got to Paris, I began talking to strangers in two languages.

I met a woman while standing in line at the cash register at the frozen food specialty store Picard; she lived in my neighborhood and we became friends. I met a woman on an airplane to Boston who turned out to live right near me. As it happened, she was seated in the wrong seat and was asked to move. We swapped cards and became friends; surely that was meant to be.

I stopped short of accepting invitations from taxi drivers, being fearful that I could take up with Mr. Goodbar. I did not pick up men. My theory is that if a man wants to meet you, he will chase you around the block. If he's not chasing you, he's not worth having.

So I limited my friendliness to women or to couples. My best accidental hunting ground for new acquaintances was in lobbies of luxury hotels. I met the most wonderful family from Morocco that I swear I will go visit one day, if I can only find where

I put their address. Maybe the most fun I had was a dinner with total strangers, who by the time we had eaten dinner seemed like old friends. I met them on the street just past the Four Seasons Hotel George V. I was walking away from the hotel, toward my bus stop, following behind a woman who was so well dressed that I couldn't help but be impressed. She was wearing the perfect travel chic ensemble—low shoes and casual clothes that were fashionable but not over the top. I felt compelled to stop her to tell her how chic she was.

She asked if I was the Born to Shop lady. I said yes, she pulled one of my books out of her tote bag and we fell into each other's arms, laughing and hugging as if we were long-lost friends. She and her husband took me to dinner a few nights later at Mon Ami Louis and we giggled and visited and ate and drank as if we'd been friends for years. Mon Ami Louis is the restaurant where Bill Clinton was entertained by the French president; this is the place where celebs and rock stars and moguls hang out because they love the dumpy atmosphere of a corner bistro from one hundred years ago (cast-iron stoves set right into the middle of the floor), but can afford to pay fifty dollars for six spears of asparagus.

The restaurant is on the edge of the fourth, close to the tenth in the most unhealthy looking block in Paris; it is virtually impossible to get a reservation with less than two weeks' notice. The concierge at the Four Seasons Hotel George V did the magic trick and won the reservation for us, but I think these strangers also had a lot of pull. We had lamb and a half bottle of a wonderful red wine and potatoes with cheesy stuff and cream that were crisp on the top. Even if I never see them again, this will be an adventure remembered as the kind of wonderful night that happens only in Paris.

35

Aside from Claire Tuttle, my most active group of friends was a bunch of five women, all interrelated by two or three degrees of separation that united us over a period of thirty years. We called ourselves Les Girls. Karen Fawcett, from BonjourParis, was our unofficial leader; she was the link that had brought us together as one. She had also lived in Paris longer than any of us, so she was our source for information, contacts and background secrets.

I am sure the five of us would have been friends anyplace in the world, anytime in our lives. Being in Paris, however, made us closer—probably because we needed an instant support system. Karen had lived in France for fifteen years at that point; Myriam had been back for three. The rest of us—Abby and Sandrine (called Sandy) and I—arrived during the same month. We were the new fish.

We all became friends or reconnected with the ones we had known years ago in a very short period, as if we didn't have the time or inclination to test each other. I'm not sure if this is because we have many things in common (two other "girls" are also widows; three of us are journalists) or because we are too old for too much foreplay. Maybe we bonded simply because what we needed was someone to really talk to and someone to really listen. These are the women I could talk to about anything: money, manners, loss, life, love, sex and constipation.

In the spring of my first year in Paris, we did things in small groups—rarely all of us together at once. We spent a lot of time e-mailing each other, sometimes hogging the screen with IMs (instant messages). There were phone calls or coffee hours spent gossiping about each other's business or idiosyncrasies. There were shopping expeditions and explorations of new sights or events, all of us hungry to devour Paris. We also informally organized our own system of sharing.

My monthly magazine collection—an enormous selection of international fashion and furnishings publications used for Born to Shop research—was recirculated among Les Girls. Myriam did group grocery shopping for all of us in London when she went to visit her daughter there. Sandy cat-sat and dog-sat and lent out her large, luxe apartment to all our friends and family. We went to movies together, swapped videotapes. I often bought specific movies and DVDs because I knew Myriam would enjoy them. We formed a community of strength.

I had told myself even before Mike actually died that I would not become a fag hag when I was single, nor would I become part of a group of widows, socializing only with middle-aged women. I was wrong. I liked these widows, these girls. I needed them. These women formed a large part of my new life; I would have been less without them. As would France.

36

I was in trouble with AOL again. The *Trésor de France,* representing the people of France through a tax system, was after me. Telecom 9, some independent phone system that I got snookered into agreeing to order because I didn't know what I was doing (it all happened in French), was still billing me, even though I had cancelled the service as soon as I discovered my error and could prove it.

My finances were a mess, I was getting notices of legal actions but I had no idea what they represented, or why, and I would swear in court that I had already paid the bills they were dunning me for. My bill-paying system was handicapped by my lack of understanding the fine degrees of the French language and the French system.

Pride also got in the way. I was very self-conscious about my need to have someone handle these things for me, but I refused to ask Claire to handle it all for me. She wouldn't accept money from me, so I felt like I was a pain in the butt to her and reserved her help for the most serious situations. Pascale-Agnès did not live in Paris, so it made no sense to have her pay my bills, although she often translated or did battle on the phone for me. Other bills I often let slip between the parquet. I was an organizational disaster.

It was not just my bad French that caused the problem. I was confused over the difference between a TIP and an RIB and the basics of bank transfer payments. I also paid bills, but paid them incorrectly and then didn't receive credit, which caused a foul ball.

The RIB (say reeb; *relevé d'identité bancaire*) was used when you contracted a service. Then, when you signed the contract for the service, you agreed to *prélèvement* (automatic payment directly from your bank account) and attached the RIB, which gave your bank the needed information for electronic payments. In most cases, the bill was paid directly from your debit account but in a few cases, it went through your Visa card. The TIP was a method of payment that did not need to be accompanied by an RIB and allowed for a one-time payment taken directly from your account.

It was all too much for me to grasp, so I have been begging Claire to open a business called either Madame Vendredi or Ma Femme Friday. I think she could make a fortune rescuing Americans who are confused by the system and need a helping hand.

37

Suddenly it was May, one of the two invisible months in France. In fact, France is the only country in the world that has only ten months in a year. August is given away to vacation time and May, well, May is filled with holidays and *ponts*.

A *pont* is indeed a bridge, but in the case of holiday time, it is a bridge over a workday created in order to provide a long weekend. When more than one day is involved, the *pont* becomes a *viaduc*. Most of the religious holidays in spring are counted off from Easter, a date that changes each year. Thus the subsequent holidays also change days and days of the week, so the system of *ponts* and *viaducs* can be very intricate.

Added to the religious holidays are things such as French Labor Day, May 1 (after which I was certain you had permission to wear white shoes) and Armistice Day. Stores closed, banks closed, mom-and-pop service businesses totally closed and all of France went *en fête*. Since I was self-employed, this didn't affect me enormously, but Paris was shutting down, and it was impossible to get any information from other people since offices were closed or deserted.

I had thankfully been booked as a geek at the Cannes Film Festival, where a TV network had asked me to lecture, give tours and provide historical background on the festival to two teams of VIPs they flew in for the two-week event.

The FIF as it is called in France (*Festival International du Film*) was originally scheduled for the first week of September in 1939. On September 1, Adolf Hitler invaded Poland. On September 2, the FIF was cancelled before it ever began. When they got back to the idea after World War II, the promoters chose the month of May in order to boost hotel occupancy in an otherwise slow month.

Through a complete accident of fate, I became an expert on the historical and trivial details of the FIF. I couldn't tell you a thing about many of the films, but I did know the odd stuff—like the fact that the first Palais de Festival in Cannes was built by a local politician who would later become famous for his need to build grand buildings—François Mitterand. I also knew that the judges saw so many movies that they could not stay awake unless they chewed gum. I knew the original location of the famed Bleu Bar, which no longer existed. I learned a lot of this nonsense because I used to give lectures on board cruise ships, and the more I went to the FIF, the more people I met, the more silly things I observed and the better the lectures became.

I have often thought that if I had to trace back the origin of the notion of moving to France, it would be related to the city of Cannes. In the early 1990s I was booked by Cunard to do a series of lectures and tours for some of their cruise ships; many of the ports of call were on the French Riviera. I was afraid I'd lose the gig if I confessed that I hadn't been to the Riviera in three years and was not au courant on the latest in spots. There was no time to fly there to brush up on Topless Shopping 101. By coincidence, a hotel manager I worked with in Brussels,

Richard Duvauchelle, was at the same time transferred back to Cannes, his hometown, where he had previously been the general manager of the Martinez, one of the city's palace hotels.

This time around, he was going to a newly opened Hilton and was trying to create a place for the Hilton in the luxury market with the city's three other older, and more famous, palace hotels. They had history and legend on their side; he had the Hilton brand name working against him, as Hilton has never been considered a luxury brand in a jet-set resort town. In short, he needed all the help he could get. But then, so did I. We made a deal—he would help me with my tours if I would give him the luncheon business, which awarded him the status of having won the Cunard account.

Our tours and luncheons became so famous that they were written up in the newspapers, were filmed for CNN and put both of us firmly into the cruise business for a few years. (The mayor of Cannes even came to some of our events.) Because of our back-scratching arrangement, I had inside information and access to materials outsiders could not get their hands on, so when Crystal Cruises came to Cannes for the fiftieth anniversary of the FIF, I was there to lecture the ship's passengers and provide many extra perks. This sealed my industry association with the event and each year after that I was usually invited to join the show. Although I do not have blond hair, a large bosom or even a very curvy figure, I became a regular on the red carpet and began to know a lot of people in Cannes.

As I hurried up La Croisette, the main beachside drag of Cannes, I was pushing against human traffic as I fought to get to my event. I was slowed down by the fact that on my arms, wrists and even between my fingers were thirty-two Yves Saint Laurent gift bags, each teeming with samples for my guests. The sidewalks were as crowded as Times Square on New Year's Eve. I had to put my head down to my chest and just push ahead. While I was in that unglamorous position, I heard a French-accented voice that rang above the crowd, "*Allo, Su-see!*" I looked up and saw one of my old friends from Cannes, pushing himself into the human highway in the opposite direction as he grinned and waved at me.

I beamed when I saw him. It was a special moment for me, because I was on the inside with him, not the outside like all the others pushing past us. I have always thought that when you bump into people you know on the street, you are no longer a tourist. I looked across La Croisette to the sea, where light bounced in patches of patterns, and I felt the sun on my bare arms and I knew throughout my whole being that I was home. Home in France, where I belonged.

38

With this kind of social life, it was inevitable that I too would be hosting dinner parties, cramming as many people as possible around my Parisian dining room table. I had a rotating parade of guests: Aaron and his friends, the Tuttles for family Sunday dinners, other journalists, visitors from out of town and even real networking-style dinner parties where I mixed and matched the guests and used place cards to maximize the business and personal connections that could be made.

I have never been very interested in cooking—it's my theory that whether or not the dinner is good, everyone eats it up, tells you it was great and then leaves you with the dishes. Even with help in the kitchen, the rewards never seem to outweigh the effort. Add to this basic philosophy the fact that many of my friends in France were not only seriously interested in serious food, but were usually hoteliers, chefs or food writers. These were not the kind of people who were going to be impressed by my skills with the skillet.

Ya gotta have a gimmick I told myself, and almost immediately decided that I would do two different styles of meals—market basket dinners, where everything came fresh from the market and I cooked very little, and American meals, often made with ingredients unavailable in Paris. Since I was in the United States often in order to see my son, it wasn't too hard to bring back unusual food specialties, from bagels to brisket.

Market basket dinners, a concept I had developed on day trips to the south of France for cruise passengers, were mostly reserved for Americans visiting Paris—people who wanted to see my apartment and be able to tell their friends back home that they relieved the tedium of one stars and magazine perfect bistros by going to the home of a real live person who actually lived in Paris. Because I lived near the marché Poncelet, one of the most famous street markets in Paris, I could tool over there with my wheely cart and load up on the kind of fixings that made an interesting dinner table, always emphasizing what was in season, what was unusual to an American and what took as little work as possible on my part.

Cooking American-style was a little trickier in France, not only because of the lack of ingredients, but because of the metric measurements and the odd oven temperatures of my strange German creature. The first few months in France, I kept forgetting to bring over an American measuring cup, which made the metric thing even harder. Needless to say, I left all my American cookbooks in the United States because it seemed pretty stupid to bring them to the gastronomy capital of the world (sorry, Italy) because the measurement system would be off. As a result, I was making American-style meals from memory, with a mixture of American, French and international ingredients as available. I had underestimated the importance of culinary novelty in Paris and could well have used those cookbooks.

My first successes were with Tex-Mex since I brought back a lot of the ingredients from San Antonio and from the famous Delicious Tamale Factory. You can get El Paso brand ingredients in most gourmet markets in Paris. When I couldn't find cheddar cheese, I substituted French cheeses—which is to say I thought the Roquefort enchiladas were inspired, but not something I plan to make again. (Okay, they sucked.)

Typical dessert at my house was brownies made from Betty Crocker brownie mix with a plop of crème frâiche on top. I also liked to make a chocolate batter from an American mix, then bake it in madeleine tins and dip the tiny pastries in chocolate yogurt. When you came to my house, you always got a taste of America twisted into the shape of France.

39

In 1998 in Cannes, I went to my first social event where English was not spoken. Even those who could speak English were speaking French. It was a fiftieth birthday party for a friend: a rather boisterous affair, complete with a dancing girl who popped out of a cake and an after-the-party party at a disco that lasted until four A.M. At dinner I sat next to a friend who I knew spoke English, so I was able to communicate and have fun. As the night and the wine wore on, after the dancing girl and the cake and the toasts, various guests got up, toasted the birthday guest and then told a joke. I learned that the telling of jokes after dinner was a common French practice.

One night after I moved to Paris, I was invited to Gerard and Marie-Jo's house for a small dinner party. English was not spoken. I managed okay. After the coffee, the joke telling began and I tensed, wondering if I would know when to laugh. But I was lucky. This is the joke I heard.

James Bond walked into a bar and ordered a martini, stirred not shaken. He noticed there was a beautiful young woman who sat alone at the other end of the bar. Nonetheless, he frequently looked down at his watch when he was not giving her the eye.

As she was leaving, the woman came up to him and said, "Are you expecting someone or can I join you? You look at your watch constantly."

"Please join me," said Bond, who then explained that he looked at his watch because it could predict the future.

"That's ridiculous," scoffed the young woman. "Tell me something your watch says."

Bond replied with his famous smile, held the watch up to his ear and announced, "My watch says you are not wearing knickers."

"That's ridiculous," said the woman again. "Of course I am wearing knickers!"

Bond raised the watch to his ear, shook it and then shook his head sadly. "Ah," he said, "my watch is running fast."

Who said the French don't have a sense of humor?

On a return trip from the United States, I decided to devote one piece of luggage to bringing back some of Mike's things, to have them with me to give me comfort in Paris. I had given away most of Mike's clothing in the days right after he died—quickly—I didn't want to look at it. But I kept the really good things and there were items that warmed my heart when I opened the closet doors and saw them hanging there. I felt that this buzz was worth the one-hundred-dollar price tag for one piece of extra luggage on the airplane, so I packed Mike's sports jackets, his white dinner jacket—which has a great story that goes with it—some ties and a few other things. I was happy to have them.

When I got back to the apartment, I unpacked them and put them in the guest room closet, where I also keep my out-of-season clothes. I was horrified to see that they took up more than one foot of hanging space in the closet. Emotional comfort is one thing, but twelve inches of hanging space in a crowded Paris apartment is, well, twelve inches of hanging space . . . and the man was dead for heaven's sake, *dead.*

But I couldn't get rid of the clothes. In fact, I still have them. I use them as a barometer. The day will come when I need the hanging space more than I need the crutch. Then I will know I have made another big step forward.

When I first got to Paris, not only did I not know anything about *le monte-charge*, but when I bought my sofa, my saleswoman never once said to me anything like "Honey, why don't you consider *le monte*?"

Le monte is the system by which furniture is delivered into French apartments by means of an outdoor lift that deposits items through a window. The process sounded terrifying and expensive to me, but *le monte* is one of those things you dread in life that turn out to be quite fine after all. To avoid frustrations and headaches with large deliveries, or an entire move, it's probably worthwhile to just book it and not worry about it. The charge more than pays for itself in ease. (*Monte-charge* for one sofa, about two hundred dollars.)

Yes, of course I measured before I bought the sofa. I measured the wall. I did not know to, or how to, measure the turns in a stairwell . . . or how to measure the mental agility of any specific moving man who may or may not be able to do the imaginary origami it takes to get a bulky piece of furniture to fit through the eye of a needle. In short, it never even dawned on me that the sofa might not fit into the front door of the apartment building, let alone up the stairwell.

I had planned to live without a sofa and a formal "living room," as in my experience, no one ever goes in the living room anyway and space in Paris is too precious to waste. But early efforts at entertaining were real efforts since people seemed to stand around with their arms crossed and a stiffness that made me nervous. I did need a sofa.

So I walked into Galeries Lafayette, deciding that one thousand dollars was my budget for a sofabed. I happen to hate sofabeds, but they only cost about one hundred dollars more than the same model in a nonsofabed version, so I figured what the hell. I chose an off-white jacquard cotton with a small prayer that my son—and guests—would not get my sofa dirty. I was tired of buying things I hated in order to have quick delivery and figured if I had been willing to live life without a sofa at all, I would be willing to wait three months for delivery of the model I really liked.

Three months later, in early June, the sofa delivery was attempted. That is to say, I stood on the curb in front of my building with the sofa and a giant man who seemed to think that just because I didn't speak French I was deaf and dumb. He just kept shrieking at me, "*C'est impossible!*"

Making rolling motions with my hands and wrists, I tried to explain that if he rolled the arm portion into the door first, and rotated the sofa body, it would work. He would have none of it and never even tried.

That sleepless night I realized that the front door to the building was actually just the beginning of problems the unjolly giant could not yet imagine . . . it was an event that merely opened Pandora's box. There were more doors after the *porte d'entrée*, a foyer (with a supporting column in the center) to my part of the building, two flights of stairs—as well as a pretty sharp turn from inside the door to my apartment through my hall and into the living room. Pass the antacid, please.

Frustrated with my lack of linguistic skill and the entire situation, I turned it over to Claire who began to whisper the m-word to me as she bravely took over. Le *monte-charge*, she said, was the way to go. It sounded a little dirty to me, and I wished she said I got Yves Monte Charge in the bargain, but her words had the practical ring to them of one who knew. Since I had already *monté les escaliers* (climbed the stairs) at the Cannes Film Festival, I decided I was ready for the next *monte* challenge.

Claire measured walls, halls, windows and doors. She faxed; she consulted; she pleaded; she translated. It was finally understood by all parties that the sofa was enormous, that I had unwittingly—in French, of course—ordered a larger size to be made in a custom order—and I was stuck with it.

Two days before the *monte-charge* date, I watched the *méteo* (weather report) on TV, praying for rain to break the heat. I then realized that I was asking for rain on the day of my *monte*. *Eeeeek*. To make a seven-foot story short, despite the fact that I needed half a tranquilizer and a mega Tagamet, the whole thing took ten minutes, was fascinating . . . and lots of fun. It changed my life.

The process was, uh, a breeze.

- One man came to my door, asked for the window of choice and strapped a large wood board, like a table-top, to it.
- Another man set up the machine downstairs in the courtyard. It was a modern version of a medieval catapult but with a ladder and platform; an open-air dumbwaiter without pulleys, run by electricity from my apartment.

- The sofa—all wrapped in industrial plastic—was loaded onto the platform and in seconds was racing up to my balcony.

The two men then pulled her (Claire and I named her Rosemary Récamier) into the apartment, cut off the plastic and placed her where indicated. They gave me a lesson in how to do the sofabed, made me try it myself, then sent the cushions up the catapult and rearranged them after I got it wrong.

I gave them each a can of Coca-Cola and thanked them profusely in bad French. "*C'est normal,*" the headman said with a Gallic shrug.

Maybe normal for him, but not for me. I just don't know why he left through my front door and didn't take the *monte* machine back down.

42

Sales in France are regulated by the government and are allowed only twice a year; all other events are "promotions." The July sales often start in the end of June; the January sales start any time from Epiphany (January 6) to a date after Epiphany, like January 15.

That, of course, is the official story. The real trick, however, was to live here and be in the know—I mean, in the know in terms of knowing people. Just because the sales dates were officially proclaimed by the government does not mean that there wasn't a little action going on beforehand. For the most part, a customer who shopped in the same stores and used the same salespeople, who built up a reputation as a good customer, was allowed to choose items to be held for the sale. One could even bargain a little, especially when multiple purchases were involved.

You could try the clothes on, even pay for them (at the reduced price), but you didn't take them home until the first day of the sale. Otherwise, it would be cheating.

43

My husband, Mike, was in the sports information business for eighteen of our twenty-five years together. I should have realized that some of it would rub off on me. For the most part, one of the rules of our marriage was that I didn't talk to him about shopping and he didn't talk to me about sports. But there had been some osmosis going on.

Once in Paris, I began to put sporting events on the television, basically only to hear them as background noise. The announcers' voices were very soothing to me; they told me all was right in the world. It didn't matter what language they were speaking. I found comfort there.

And so, completely by accident, I got hooked on the Europe Cup *football* (soccer) play-offs and finals that filled the spring airwaves and went through the month of June. While I never learned too much about soccer when I was a Westport soccer mom (I thought going to the games was a social event to see the other parents), I did figure it out in France—it's sort of like basketball. Easy. The guys go up the field and down the field and sometimes they kick the ball into that netty thing, a different variety of a hoop. Got it.

I began watching play-off games at home, by myself, planning my evenings around the games and kick-off. I learned not only all the team members' names, but what they looked like, where they were from and where they lived (many dodge French taxes by living elsewhere). I had a favorite (Barthez). I began shouting instructions (in English) to the French team, especially since they seemed to need so much help from me. Without question, this French team played badly throughout most of the round robin games and then, in every single game, somehow won in the last seconds. It was truly an amazing phenomenon.

French friends became so impressed with my acumen that I was actually invited to a French-speaking party for the very last game, the championship, and warned that they took this very seriously and it was not a social event. I bought a boy's-size French soccer suit from a street vendor (no adult sizes), threw out the little blue shorts and then hand-beaded the T-shirt, which said FRANCE. I wore the beaded T-shirt with a pair of tight white jeans and high heels to the party. I screamed "*allez*" whenever France had the ball.

In fact, I had unwittingly absorbed so much at my husband's side during televised sports events, that I knew a good play from a bad one and good luck from bad luck. I could even translate these into French and defend my position that the team sucked, they were just lucky. Thank God they had me to explain it all to them.

I decided that now that I was on the team, so to speak, that for the next year's season I would treat myself to a Saint Germain Paris team T-shirt because it says SG PARIS on it—this being my personal logo. And me being very much a member of the team.

44

Of course, for the most part, the French didn't want an American opinion on how to play ball . . . or anything else. Didn't want; didn't need—to their way of thinking anyway. I'd done enough consulting to French businesses to realize that most French people were simply closed to ideas from outsiders. Actually, they are pretty much closed to new ideas, period. Ideas from outsiders were not even worth the breath they took to be expressed.

A French person would never tell you to shut up or go away; that would be rude. The French really are never rude. More in keeping with the national character would be to tell you that you are a genius, that your ideas are brilliant . . . and to then ignore you and your fabulous ideas. I learned all this the hard way.

For the most part, they told me I was clever and they ignored—and disdained—me. Yet one day, shock of shocks, an idea was enthusiastically accepted. My task had been to create a Paris-themed souvenir. I made a model of the product; the group to which I presented it was so excited (*mon dieu!*) that they began production phone calls right then in front of me while the meeting was still in progress. They asked me what colors the item should be made in.

"Why, red, white and blue, of course," I said without hesitation.

Silence blanketed the group of eight people. Dumb looks all around. I repeated myself in French. Still no reaction. Then a full minute later, some whispering and a rumble of reaction.

"Ah, blue, white and red!" said a Frenchman, finally understanding.

I'll never forget the point. It was cultural; all in the wrist.
American children are taught that the flag is red, white and blue
and tend to repeat this color group in that order—even as adults.
French children learn their flag is *bleu, blanc et rouge*—blue,
white and red—and only understand these same colors when
named in *that* order.

Every day I learned a small, stupid and essential detail.

45

Many outsiders do not understand the simple differences in culture and lifestyle in France . . . or the French way of thinking.
They invariably go home with stories of those quaint little
Frenchies. Those who are able to adjust are changed forever and
usually choose to stay, or to return when possible.

The pace of life in France is different. For me, used to a
rather hectic American day, it was a relief when I slowed down
and actually enjoyed my life in the French style. I had been the
person who ate a peanut butter and jelly sandwich over the keyboard. I never had time to cook; my family survived on take-
out, fast food, Boston Chicken and lamb chops on Sunday
nights. Suddenly meals and social life were the most important
parts of my day. Yes, more important than my work. In France
they were the anchors to a day and to a lifetime. In the United
States, we rarely made time for our friends and the people we
cared most about—and they understood this, or said they did,

because they were in the same jam. In France nothing was more important.

In France people sat at table for three hours (or longer), ate slowly and had real conversations. This contrasted with an eat-and-run American pattern or even the "independent dinners" we had in our family because everyone had different activities and different needs. Other than Thanksgiving, Jewish holiday feast dinners and a few dinners out with friends, I don't remember sitting at table for much more than an hour in the United States . . . or having discussions about politics and philosophy.

People in France made less money than those in the United States but still lived better—partly because of this slower pace of life, partly because of the cultural importance of a good meal (with good wine, *bien sûr*) and partly because, with less discretionary income, priorities were better defined. If a French person had to choose between new clothes or a concert ticket, the concert ticket usually won out.

Add to this a thirty-five-hour workweek, a schedule of a mere two hundred workdays per year, some six or eight weeks of paid vacation, socialized medical care, excellent retirement benefits and a cost of living far lower than Manhattan or London and you can see why people loved to live here. Those who knew what they couldn't afford back in the United States figured they'd rather have less in France and chose to stay put. While my original idea was to stay in France for a year to "get it out of my system," instead I found that I liked the French lifestyle better than the one I could have had back in the United States. Although a low dollar forces me to cut back, that's easier to do in France.

46

Despite my active social life, there were evenings that I just wanted—indeed, needed—to stay at home. I took off my makeup, pulled my hair back, put on one of Mike's shirts, ate dinner in bed and watched TV. It was almost heaven. *C'est paradis, ça.*

The news comes on at 8 P.M. the weather at 8:45 and then prime time begins at either 8:50 or 8:55. Programming is done at odd hours since the commercial breaks are not at regularly set intervals as in America. Most people use the commercials for going to the bathroom or making phone calls; I like the adverts. I'm also still green enough to be amazed at the amount of nudity in them and the down-to-earth human frailties used to sell products: childbirth; pet droppings; annoying houseguests and relatives; and sex in and out of showers, sofas and beds.

The shows are a mix of French products and international imports—mostly American TV movies and series. To choose a prime-time show that has been dubbed from American TV, you have to be able to translate the French title to the American one. The names in French are rarely direct translations of the show's name in English and with police shows, they are so similar to each other that you can quickly become confused. Most of the newer series are on cable stations, but network French TV does have *Le Caméléon* (*The Pretender*), *Alerte à Malibu* (*Baywatch*) and *High Secret City* (*Picket Fences*). The crime-buster Las Vegas–based hit *CSI* came to France almost immediately after it began in the United States, but the title here is *Les Experts*. I found *Law & Order* by accident when I tuned into what I thought was a tribute to the city of New York after September 11 since the program was named *Special Unité NY*. Surprise, madame.

Cable television has more of these American series than the French networks; some of these shows are even in English. But I am trying to perfect my French, so I'd rather watch *Who Wants to Be a Millionaire*. They not only speak French, but print the questions on the screen so you can see how the words are pronounced.

I tend to watch French *policiers* (police shows) because there's a lot of action so I can guess what's happening when I don't understand the words. One night, I watched in amusement as the French policemen stopped not for donuts but éclairs, then fought over who got the chocolate one and who got the coffee-flavored.

Take that, Dunkin' Donuts.

47

I think there is a place in the grieving process where you suddenly move forward a giant step; with this move comes some sort of self-improvement phase. I imagine it is the acceptance that you are going to live after all, that as much as you wished it, the earth was unable to open and swallow you, that you are forced to go on . . . and that to go on requires strength.

I suddenly wanted to be physically stronger.

Accordingly, out of the blue, I felt a compulsion to join a gym, do exercises and get on a treadmill. Okay, okay, there was a tiny bit of socialization in the notion; I did think that if I joined the right gym I might meet some interesting people or make some new friends and thought it would get me out of the house and keep me active. Sitting at the café could hardly be described as exercise (even in France).

My husband was a big believer in the daily workout. Mike went to a small gym in Westport in order to get stronger and help control his weight, but he soon found another family there—indeed, his trainer and many of the coaches from the gym were at his funeral. He was always after me to join up; for gift-giving occasions he wanted to give me sessions with a personal trainer. I wanted clothes, shoes, handbags, jewelry, candles, tole trays, pashmina, Chanel. The gym?

My idea of exercise in those days was to walk up and down the aisles of TJ Maxx or stride from store to store in a two-million-square-foot shopping mall. When the exercise obsession hit me in Paris, I was really embarrassed, with that kind of inner chuckle you get when you realize how much life has changed . . . how much you have changed. Mike would have been so pleased to see me go to a gym . . . and so shocked.

To me, one of the most interesting aspects of my sudden desire to work out was that the urge was in no way related to my thickening figure or my need to lose ten kilos.

I really, really wanted to improve my posture, to have military posture. I wanted arms like Madonna and thighs of steel. I craved strength. I wanted to be faster than a speeding TGV train. I wanted to leap tall buildings, including the Eiffel Tower, in a single bound. I had chosen life, dammit, and I needed to be ready for anything.

At the same time that I became crazed with my need for biceps, I read in a French magazine that you could join the gym at the Ritz as a private club, for about three thousand dollars a year. I dreamed of the Pamela Harriman Memorial Swimming Pool and all the Arabian princes I would meet during my workout. I knew that if Princess Diana was still alive we would be doing squats together. Then I remembered that I hate to get my hair wet, hardly ever go swimming and that Arabian princes have little interest in Jewish princesses. I also admitted to myself that I was terrible at getting out my door and into a gym; that I was capable of paying a lot of money for something and then thinking up excuses to not use it.

Then Karen Fawcett (of Les Girls and BonjourParis) introduced me to Martine Curtis-Oakes, a woman from San Francisco who with her husband had recently moved to Paris. Martine was a Pilates instructor who had a studio and spa, but would then come to your home for a private session. Bingo!

I signed up for two sessions a week. I cannot tell you I became a zealot, or that Olga Korbut has anything to worry about, but I now have a routine of stretching exercises that I do daily almost without fail. (I said almost.) Later in the year, I added weight training.

A few months after a girlfriend in Atlanta was widowed, I went to visit her. We talked and compared mental health notes. "So," I asked her, "have you booked a trainer yet?"

She burst out laughing. "How did you know?"

I explained that I was convinced that all widows pass through certain rites of passage—redecorating being only one of them. The need for an exercise class, a private trainer or a series of regular repetitions seems almost written into the genetic code of grief.

When I did my workout routines, I often thought about the

move to Paris and the changes in my life. I was very aware that I was no longer the person I used to be, that I had a new lifestyle and new habits, and that each time I reached I was reaching for my future. I was forcing myself to be stronger.

48

When Mike was dying, I thought the thing I would miss the most was my best friend, having someone to talk to who understood me so well. As it turned out, the single thing I missed most was being held.

I'm not talking about sex. I missed sex, but being held—especially in a nonsexual way—just as support, is so important that sometimes I do not know how to cope without it. I yearned to find rescue—or simply peace—in my husband's embrace. I called several of my single girlfriends for advice, to see if they too craved the comfort.

Maggie said that she booked a massage once a week, just for the touch therapy.

Monique said she had a vibrator. I explained that wasn't what I meant, but that while we were on the subject—a subject few people cared to discuss—I had a vibrator that was a gift but I didn't know how to use it.

"Ah," said Monique, "this is something every Frenchwoman knows. You must learn. It takes practice. It is very important for when you need to scream and scream."

49

I was able to take a leave from my publishing deadlines when my husband was diagnosed and during the immediate transition period into widowhood and France. By late spring, however, I felt ready to get back to work for Born to Shop.

I went to Hong Kong, Beijing and Shanghai—trips filled with reunions with old friends; good food; good memories; and fabulous shopping. While I normally travel alone, on this trip two friends accompanied me because they were worried about me and thought this was an appropriate gesture of support for a widowed friend. One companion was a girlfriend from San Antonio, also a widow. The other was a Chinese friend who insisted I needed a translator and protector. They were bookends to my grief and a circle of strength as I started back to work.

As smooth as the trip went, there was something spiritual about my return home to Paris. Suddenly, within my skin and my furnishings, I was more settled than in the first six months of the year. It took going away in order to feel at home. I looked around my living room, newly arranged to accommodate my Chinese finds, surveyed my kingdom and felt pleased with myself. I was at home, snug as a bug in a needlepoint carpet bought at the Friendship store for $499. Ah Mike, how did this happen to me?

When I walked around my *quartier,* especially the first few days back in town, I had a giddy sense of being in Paris . . . made more silly with the realization that Paris *was* my home. I walked the avenue Niel, a residential and commercial street around the corner from my apartment that rarely sees tourists, and marveled anew at the shapes of the apartment buildings, the wrought iron on the balconies, the heavy, hand-carved wooden doors, the tumble of geraniums. I might have chosen this neighborhood by pure accident, but my God, I chose well. Or lived under a lucky French star. I had no power over my husband's fate, but I had made some good choices in beginning my new life.

I went to Auchan at La Defense for a big-haul shopping to restock the apartment. Instead of going into the mall directly from the train station as I normally did—I went up the escalator to the Grande Arche, one of François Mitterand's *grands travaux* (landmark projects). It was the first time I actually stood under it.

In fact, I had never seen the Grande Arche in person until I moved to Paris. Then I saw it by accident. I was taking a taxi to meet a friend at the Marriott Hotel on the Champs Elysées. But the taxi driver got mixed up and headed out toward Le Meridien. As he shot around l'Étoile, ahead of me I saw the Grande Arche and behind me I saw the Arc de Triomphe. I was stunned. I suddenly understood it all. Ridicule Mitterand and his building projects if you must; I am filled with respect.

In Paris, unlike in many other cities, architecture is more than beauty. Its strength lies not just in concrete and steel or Roman building techniques, but in the emotional grip it has on people. I stood there, bending my head back and looking upward in awe. I let the power of architecture and time and place sweep me away and let tears flow down my cheeks. I tilted my face up toward the arch and the sky of France. *Vive la France*, I said to myself and then went inside to do the grocery shopping.

50

Long ago I became convinced that some of my attraction to France was based on its physical size, as well as the size of the population. France has a population of about 60 million souls. The United States is almost five times larger at 289 million. France is not only a small country, but it *feels* exactly the right size to me.

Something in my sensory system is in tune with the aspects of size as a comfort zone, or personal space taken to a national recognition factor. In a population of 60 million people, you know who all the players are. I found myself with a strong sense of self. In America's large population, it's harder to find your way and to make your own place. I had often felt lost in America; even lost in Manhattan. In Manhattan if you are not young and rich and hot to trot, you are invisible. If you get to be my age, and you are neither rich nor famous, you are equally invisible. In France, you could find a place at anyone's dinner table if you were interesting.

As an American who stepped into this new world, I think I was able to adjust more easily than some because I have always had an interest in history and a passion for a way of life that is all but gone from the United States. My university degree is in history; my favorite books are historical fiction and historical biography. I am truly interested in how life was lived in the past, which, believe it or not, provides information for daily life in modern France.

I have a personal theory that many of the Americans who like living in France share an inner craving to return to a way of life from times past; they don't mind that many things in France don't work . . . that France is behind the times in just about everything. They prefer the slow pace and the social structure of another era. The trade-offs are worth it. Sure, these expats have mobile phones and computers and enjoy modern modem life, but they are also offended by the hustle and bustle of a world of yield management, crime in the home as well as on the streets, drive-by shootings and corporate unaccountability without employer loyalty for the working guy.

France is a small, socialized state. Many of these problems don't exist. Many of the problems that do exist aren't reported on the news. To live in France is to return to an almost medieval way of thinking, doing business and even talking. Translate some words from French and what do you get? The number eighty means "4 twenties"; to say please, one actually says the words "if it pleases you" and when you say you're welcome, you are really saying "to you I pray." This is an old-fashioned world dressed in the clothes of the twenty-first century, but not really in tune with it.

It's my bet that expats also like the challenge of things being a little bit harder within the structure of their lives; they are as tough as pioneers and can take the stress of doing business—and living life—in a different code. They like the rules and the manners; they like the quaint thinking that passes as marketing in France. They like a country that is about bad television and good magazines and even better conversation.

Ever since the success of women's lib, there have been magazine articles and newspaper features about women who have reached the top, then turned around and given it up to be stay-at-home mommies or to simply quit the rat race. In my own way, I was one of them: The Runaway Widow. The Start-Again Lady. If I had it all, I left it all.

I was far more impressed, however, with the story of a woman I once knew named Carole Wallace. We worked together at *People* magazine over twenty years ago. Carole rose to the top of the tower and became the managing editor. One day, she up and quit—she gave appropriate notice and guided her team through a transition—then moved to a small village in Scotland where I have heard she runs an inn with a spa. She is living the Bob Newhart show in real life, but with a foot in two different centuries. She traded big for small; fast for slow.

It doesn't have to be in France or Scotland, but it's my guess that a lot of Baby Boomers will find the rat race overrated and the *confiture* overseas to be underrated. They will quit an insensitive way of life to find something better whether in the United States or Europe.

Carole Wallace and I have found it already.

 # Summer

The Gallery, Four Seasons Hotel George V, 8e
Pour boire: thé glacé parfumé

Summer was a time of invitations to the French countryside, of hot days in Paris, made lazy by no air-conditioning and the fact that just about everyone was on vacation. By early August the city took on a ghost town aura—deliciously empty. I bought my first pair of shorts—only worn inside my apartment, of course—and pulled my hair back in a pony-tail, to keep it off my neck. When I went out and about, I wore long, baggy linen dresses and a straw hat. All of Paris relaxed the rules.

I no longer went to a café every day because of my out-of-town invitations, but when in Paris, I became a regular at The Gallery in the lobby of the Four Seasons Hotel George V. The George V reopened at about the same time that I moved to Paris, so we were sort of related. The posh hotel was air-conditioned; they served great iced tea (which was just becoming popular in Paris) and yet The Gallery had a cafélike atmosphere where you could eat lunch, have tea or cocktails or just sit around with the newspaper.

The Gallery was made for writing in my notebook while admiring the handiwork of the hotel's creative director, Jeff Leatham, who was fast becoming one of the most famous Americans in Paris, celebrated for his imaginative floral creations. Crowds of tourists came by to gawk, but I just sat in my armchair and scribbled in my notebook.

Hmmph, *I would think to myself,* these damn tourists.

51

It was the summer of *thé glacé parfumé,* the French version of iced tea. Iced tea was new to France and based on the addition of French fruit or flower *sirops.* The French tea party was created by the use of natural ingredients, some of which even had the aroma of summer right in the bottle. Sometimes there was one fruit essence in the mix, other times, a duo such as apple–cherry, apricot-nectarine or green apple–vanilla. At the bar of the Four Seasons Hotel George V in Paris, the iced tea itself was fruit flavored, in accordance with the chef's move toward desserts made of fruits and flowers and the hotel's design effort to provide the most dramatic floral backdrop in Paris.

Of course, summer in Paris wasn't truly chic—because of the weather (it could be winter one day and summer the next) and the fact that few buildings were air-conditioned, so that when it was hot, it was hot. Those buildings that were air-conditioned had rather inefficient cooling systems. Women wore short-sleeved suits to work and, of course, went without stockings. Fake tans were just catching on, so you often saw a woman with a naturally tanned or even a sunburned upper torso and orange streaked legs. Many Frenchwomen not only still smoked, but still took the sun, feeling a tan now was more important than any considerations of middle age or health.

It was so hot that I was forced to retreat to my favorite shoe discounter (Moda, 79 rue des Victoires, 9e; metro: Chaussée d'Antin) where I bought six pairs of sandals and slides, since none of my other shoes were comfortable without hosiery. I had to invent a new fashion statement for myself in order to be cool enough to cope. I bought pressed powder for the first time; I carried a bottle of water with me so I could rehydrate. I walked more slowly. Summer in France caused me to shift gears; I became a living definition of the word *languid*.

52

Maybe there was something in the air that July . . . or in the iced tea. There was undeniably a voice that whispered *it's been six months since Mike died, she can begin to date*. Something happened inside me, as if there was some kind of internal clock. *Bong.* Friends commented on it and asked if I was ready to meet men; one French friend clapped his hands together, dusted them apart and announced "So! It is six months now! You must take a lover!"

Even the actual six-month anniversary of Mike's death was a holiday, July 4, a day of celebration and fireworks. My father was practically remarried six months after my mother died; I had yet to go on a date.

I read the personals in *FUSAC*, the expat magazine with adverts for everything from used refrigerators to gay liaisons. I had read the personals in the back of *New York* magazine for years, just because I find them amusing. The *FUSAC* ads all began with JH, and since almost everyone in *New York* magazine who advertises is Jewish and says so in the ads, I thought this mean *juif homme*, Jewish man. But there was a disproportionate number of

JHs; I knew there weren't that many Jews in France. It wasn't adding up. I finally realized that JH meant *jeune homme*, young man. (Besides, a Jewish man would be *homme juif*, not vice versa.)

I told this *FUSAC* story to a Jewish woman I knew who promptly mailed me a small newspaper named *Tribune Juive*. She had turned it inside out so that facing forward were the back pages called *"Entre Nous"* where the personal ads were posted. These ads did not have to say the subjects were Jewish, that was taken for granted. Instead, the ads explained what kind of Jewish—either with the abbreviation *ash.*, meaning Ashkenazi, or of Eastern European decent—or *seph.* for Sephardic. If they were seeking *une dame religieuse,* she better already have several sets of dishes for keeping kosher. Many of the adverts were for middle-aged people; there were also ads from several marriage brokers. The ads were gently written; many were charming, but I didn't think I was ready to have a date with someone who probably did not speak English.

So my first actual date was with Stanley; Stanley from Syracuse I called him. I had been hearing about Stanley from Syracuse since I moved to France. No, before. Since a few days after Mike died.

My parents lived in Syracuse, New York, when they were first married. I was born there—as were my siblings. We moved away when I was eight, but my parents stayed in touch with their group of friends. Word spread that I was widowed. Messages began to arrive insisting that I had to be connected with Stanley, Stanley from Syracuse, a man who kept a nice apartment in Paris, was single, rich, creative and the nicest guy in the world . . . a perfect match, everyone said, just perfect.

Stanley called from the States to book our date. Good, I like advance planning. He invited me to see his apartment, have a drink and then go to dinner. I had expected this type of invitation since he lived way across Paris from me and when people had conversations about Stanley from Syracuse, they always proclaimed the wonder of his apartment overlooking the Seine. Although Paris does indeed have an excellent public transportation system, there are some neighborhoods that are simply geographically undesirable to others, like the stretch from my apartment in the northwestern part of Paris to Stanley's, on the far side of an island in the most medieval part of the center of the city. True love should blossom along direct metro or bus routes.

When he opened the door I knew he wasn't for me. Not that you can judge a man by his pate or his belly, but Stanley appeared to be my father's age and a cross between Santa Claus and Alfred Hitchcock, with some Yul Brynner and Karl Malden thrown in. Since I couldn't bolt, I stepped past the tenth-century hand-carved wooden door and embarked on my first date.

Stanley from Syracuse was certainly as rich as advertised; maybe richer to judge from his surroundings. He gave me the tour of his digs, leaving out no missed cue for the visitor to ooh and aah. The building itself dated back to the fifth century (as did Stanley, I thought); the apartment was the penthouse on three levels with raw, exposed beams, stone walls and miles of good taste dripping from the rustic beams.

"So," Stanley said, bringing me into the main salon overlooking the reflected lights on the river and raising a glass of champagne in my direction, "is your divorce final yet?"

It was all I could do to not burst out laughing. So much for

Kismet. So much for Stanley's paying attention to details. I stammered that I was a widow; Stanley covered smoothly and we drank more champagne. We made small talk about people in Syracuse I hadn't seen in forty-five years. Finally we went down to dinner at a restaurant he touted as a great little place in the neighborhood. Normally, I like those kinds of places; I'm not the type who judges a date by how expensive—or famous—the restaurant he chooses is. We headed toward La Tour d'Argent and my heart stopped; I wasn't dressed properly . . . and I wasn't at all certain I could take three hours at the table with Stanley from Syracuse, who seemed to have very little in common with me . . . or anyone born after World War II. But the idea of the famed three-star Tour d'Argent as "a little place around the corner" did amuse me and made me think perhaps I had judged Stanley too harshly, too quickly. Maybe he did have a sense of humor, after all.

We did not go to Tour d'Argent, but instead to one of those tourist places on the *quai* side of the Left Bank, the kind that had posters of Van Gogh paintings, bright blue and chrome yellow trim that was too bright and giant sunflowers painted in the windows. I cringed and realized I would rather have been taken to McDonald's or one of the zillions of fun, cheap joints in Paris— anything but a tourist trap. I'd been told how sophisticated Stanley from Syracuse was. Yeah.

If first dates were a sporting event, points would have been knocked off the total score for bad choice of restaurant and for appearing cheap, for not thinking I rated anything better than this . . . or that I didn't know the difference. Although dinner started out slowly in terms of the pace between Stanley and me, and the food was embarrassingly mediocre, something happened at one point in the meal that shifted the gears and made the rest of the evening bearable. I did not have a good time but I didn't have a bad time either. I knew that Stanley would put me in a cab; the cab fares back and forth to his apartment cost as much as my share of the dinner—a point that I thought was funny and one of the absurd notables of a crummy date. At the open door of the cab (the meter was therefore running), Stanley decided not on the polite kisses on each cheek, but a sloppy, mushy, high school smack on the lips with a little bit of grabbing at the waist, hips and bosom. In the movie version of this date, I would have slapped him. Instead, I burst out laughing. When the going gets rough, I tend to laugh.

I had the kind of evening that made me understand why my father had married so soon after my mother died. After only one date I knew the truth: dating sucked. I also knew I wanted a real beau; I wanted to be swept off my feet; I wanted a reason to shave my legs again.

53

In France, the summer is simply July and August, period. It's only July if you want to get anything done, but emotionally, summer is July and August. June was really part of the spring, but in July and August, the rules were different.

Among my American journalist friends, summer officially began immediately after the July 4 party held for us at the Hotel Meurice. The Meurice had reopened after a two-year renovation on July 4 and soon had a party that was better than anything this side of the Riviera. Dinner was in the private ballroom; there was a vaudeville show after the meal and before dessert, during which the opera singers ripped open their bodices to reveal stars and stripes.

Cocktails were served on the rooftop, part of the hotel's grandest private suite, but when drizzle began, we retreated downstairs. The rooftop suite of the Meurice was one of those places that you never got tired of staring at, so that everyone made the tour of each room, spending an especially long time in the bathroom, which was larger than my first apartment in New York. Among its many amenities was an oval Jacuzzi fitted into a window seat, so that you could sit and soak and stare at Paris beneath you. "*Pas mal,*" you could hear each person mutter. "Not bad."

All the guests were dressed up, networking like mad, and giving grand send-offs to their friends. In France it is common to say goodbye for the summer with no expectation of having any contact with your friends until fall. If your Paris crowd didn't do Deauville, it was unlikely you'd get together. Various social crowds in Paris had specific venues and retreats, but the journalists tended to have their houses all over the country and went their own way each summer. Journalists were never part of the Deauville crowd anyway, which was rich and horsey . . . and *snob,* as the French said.

"Have a nice summer!"

Kiss-kiss on each cheek.

"Will I see you in Provence?"

"Are you going Stateside in August?"

"*À bientôt,* then, *à très bientôt.*"

By two A.M., when the last air kisses were bestowed and the

final cognac shared, the summer season unofficially began. We drifted into separate taxis, in puffs of alcoholic delight with chiffon trailing and that contented feeling of knowing that you lived in Paris, that all was right in the world.

54

Then it happened. I suddenly had a boyfriend . . . if you can call a seventy-two-year-old man a boy or use the word *boyfriend* when describing a French aristocrat with the red thread of the Legion of Honor woven into his suit lapels.

We met at the U.S. Embassy in Paris at their annual July 4 cocktail bash. I was on my way to the fete at the Hotel Meurice, but popped into the embassy because Walter Wells—who was accompanying me to the Meurice since his wife, Patricia, was out of town—had an invitation and asked me along. I thought the idea of going to the embassy for the first time sounded incredibly neat, especially on July 4.

Walter, as the managing editor of the *International Herald Tribune,* knew everyone. He was quickly off with the kiss-kiss business of greeting old friends while I circled the room, looking for new friends. As I passed the knots of people, a tall, beautiful and quite elegant man spoke to me in English with a subtle British accent, "You are too beautiful to walk past me. I say a prayer you will stop to talk to me."

Have you ever in your life heard such a line?

So I flashed him my most dazzling smile and told him I've never heard such a fabulous piece of bullshit in my life. He blanched, but recovered quickly, took my arm and said, "We can only meet properly over champagne." He led me to the bar. He told me his name and then taught me how to pronounce it. He had a title. I was just American enough to be impressed.

The count and I quickly got lost in each other. Okay, I have always been a sucker for a tall, handsome man with white hair, blue eyes, a hooked nose and an accent. He was in fact French, but spoke English with a British accent because his nanny was British. He lived in Geneva. His wife lived—separately he went to pains to explain—in a château in Évian. They had grown apart. She probably didn't understand him anymore, I mused. Pity. He said he came to Paris often because there was a branch of his bank here. He owned the bank. His children were grown; he and his wife were discreet. Was I perhaps free to leave the party so we could sit at a café and get to know each other better?

This sure beats Stanley from Syracuse and that lonely architect from FUSAC, I was thinking to myself when Walter scooped me onto his arm and whisked me away to our dinner party, a few blocks away. I gave the count my business card, wondering if I would ever hear from him again.

The flowers arrived at ten the next morning.

My first thought was to rent the videotape of *Gigi*.

You may be wondering why I was contemplating an affair with a man some twenty years my senior. The answer was related to my Aunt Lynn. Aunt Lynn was widowed when she was about sixty-two; she was stunning and very well connected socially. Her phone rang constantly, but she quickly complained to me that the men who were asking her out were eighty years old, a fact that didn't amuse her one bit. She said the men her age wanted women who were forty . . . and could get them. To an eighty-year-old, a sixty-year-old woman was a hot number. She explained that the unwritten rule in these things was about twenty years.

So I understood from the get-go that I was a trophy for an older man and a has-been to anyone my own age. This was a rather terrifying thought and a philosophy that I think will fall apart as more and more Baby Boomers become widows and widowers, but for now, well, Aunt Lynn was right on the money.

And let's face it, the count seemed perfect for my needs. He was married, so this wasn't going to get too serious. He didn't live in Paris so he wasn't going to be around too much to make me nuts and he was French-born, which meant if things evolved, I would be able to do my homework assignment for the girls back home.

Yes, I came to France with homework. After Mike died and right before I left for Paris, two of my Jewish girlfriends took me to lunch to send me off properly. As goodbye gifts they gave me a package of condoms, a vibrator and instructions to have an affair with a Frenchman and send back illustrated details, since none of us had ever seen an uncircumcised male part.

And so I began a serious flirtation with a man I soon began to call the Count of Monte Cristo, since I could not reveal his real name to my friends. I called him my quasi-boyfriend, which was my way of announcing that he was married. That really didn't bother me at all. I thought adultery was a French treat I should try just like Krug or fried courgette flowers.

He called me several times a day. There was e-mail sent from a secret account. Flowers arrived on a regular basis, but never on the same day of the week and never the same flowers. They weren't even from the same florist in Paris. We whispered sweet nothings to each other on airwaves from Geneva to Paris as we told each other our past and our present and our dreams and our schedules. It became my goal to become his mistress.

I must first admit that I love the word *mistress*. I adore the very concept; it is so French. Americans don't like the word, or even understand it. In fact, I once had a dreadful professional moment when Jonas Salk called me on the phone to sternly scold me that his wife, Françoise Gilot, should not be referred to as "Pablo Picasso's former mistress."

I had written a large story on Françoise for *People* magazine, partly because I had known Jonas since my childhood and had access to this famous couple that no one else could get. Yet when it came time to close the story for *People,* Uncle Jonas was screaming at me that *mistress* was an old-fashioned word, it was demeaning, no one used a word like that anymore and that *People* magazine should come up with a more modern term. I called the main office in New York, explained the problem, they fixed it and I called back Uncle Jonas.

"New York suggested 'live-in honey.' "

"Fine."

I thought mistress was far more attractive a description than live-in honey, but as I said, I liked the word, so *Cosmopolitan* magazine, so *Breakfast at Tiffany's,* so Louis Jourdan. It's maybe even so Charles Jourdan. And since the count and I could never really set up housekeeping, I had no thoughts of becoming his live-in honey.

55

And so the season began. I watched television while I waited for the count to call. What can you say about a country where the best television show of the year—and one of the most watched—is the daily broadcast of a three-week-long, five-thousand-kilometer cross-country bicycle race?

Ma agenda Parisienne
With apologies to Helen Fielding and Bridget Jones

Paris: Month six of widowhood; month four in France
French verbs learned: 0; Frogs kissed: 2; Princes discovered: 1;
Dust balls cleared: 0; geraniums watered: 6.

Feel that since in Paris should be doing something Parisian like walking on Champs Élysées with small dog. Smoking Gauloise. Pretending to be short. Instead am in apartment watching wicked sports event and wondering how to use vacuum cleaner, called *aspirateur*. Conspirator I say; asspirator. Nothing sucks like an Electrolux, as they say.

Should be going to Prix de Diane in Chantilly or horse races at Longchamp. Do not own hat. Do not have tickets. Must dust and vacuum, if able to work bloody contraption. Must find horsey friends next year. Will hang out at Hermès this holiday season. Would love to be out on beautiful spring day, but have promised self to tidy apartment and hang pictures as decorations have not progressed, nor has cleanup.

Watching telly for cultural purposes; trying to figure out how they arrive at day's final score of these blokes on bikes and why entire country is mesmerized. Must be the tight black pants. Could be watching same race every day except scenery changes. Horses easier to understand and have better names. Will watch bikers now and dust tonight, this making me more French. Must find yellow jersey to wear. Hmm, must go shopping for yellow jersey. Maybe tight black pants too.

❦

Nowadays, most Americans know about the Tour de France, the famous bike race that lasts for three weeks and spans much of the French countryside. Twenty years ago, when I first learned about it, few except sports enthusiasts knew anything about what was considered a French cult thing. Back in those days, we lived in L.A. and our son went to a fancy school for Hollywood kids, the sort of school in a Jackie Collins novel. Among the parents were two fathers who were making a film called *The Yellow Jersey*. We bumped into them at the Hotel Meurice one July, where we joined them in front of the hotel to watch the bikers speed into Paris on the final leg. I was hooked.

For my first summer in Paris, I put on the television every day to watch the race. My fellow Texan Lance Armstrong was in the race after beating cancer. I know he pumped a little bit of the way just for Mike and everyone else who didn't make it in the race for life. Lance was right: it's not about the bike. He too was starting over.

56

They call it *le temps de cerise,* the time of cherries. Aside from this accurate description of the produce at any grocery store or street market early each summer, it is also a sort of slang expression, a handle that means "the good times" or even "the good old days," perhaps what Americans might call the salad days, although the American expression has more of a hint of nostalgia to it. Because French culture is so devoted to the seasons, *le temps de cerise* came to represent the fat days of summer when so many fruits and vegetables were in season and markets were piled high with colors and textures that begged for you to touch and squeeze and smell and taste.

While Americans have come to expect a certain regular availability of produce because of international buying and shipping and alternate seasons below the equator, in France it has never mattered if the goods were available or not; tradition was tradition, there was right and there was wrong. It truly mattered what season it was; only heathens (or Americans) ate fruits or foods out of season. Because of this unwritten law, the good times were especially appreciated for their bounty. The market basket was a symbol of summer.

My first *temps de cerise* in France will always be remembered for the seduction in the air, the promise of a love affair with the count, the wonder of constant invitations to different parts of France where after a simple train ride I was ushered into another world of secrets to learn. *Le temps* meant the delicious pace of working only half days and taking long siestas, naked under French milled sheets, with French doors open to the light and the hint of a breeze.

It was all put into place the day a liveried messenger came to my door with a large hand-painted faience bowl, filled with tiny, fresh, juicy apricots. There was no note, but I knew they were from the count. I don't even like apricots, but the beauty of the color and their voluptuous teasing made me smile. Life in France was more than a bowl of cherries; *le temps de cerise* was about more than fruit.

57

I decided to accept Karen Fawcett's invitation to a few days at her home in Provence. I also thought that playing a little bit hard to get was a good approach with the count. I should be busy. He should send more flowers. Mangoes would be nice. He should have trouble finding me via telephone . . . or I should be in a situation where I had to tell him it was rude to talk on the portable. He should think there was a big demand on my time and attention. He should chase me so I could let him catch me.

Karen and her husband, Victor Kramer, had chosen northern Provence for their second home. They lived outside a village between Orange and Vaison-la-Romaine. Pat and Walter Wells began the American migration to this part of the Vaucluse when they bought their vineyard in Vaison, way before there were any other Americans around. Karen and Victor were early arrivals; their house was already twelve years old that summer. Now the region was filled with expats: friends and fans of the Wells's as well as assorted journalists who moved in following the Wells's lead, wanting to enjoy the combination of low real estate prices, great markets, cheap wine and other newshounds with whom to discuss the meaning of life, or life in France.

Karen gave me instructions for my train ticket to Orange, but she told me to buy a first class ticket. I told her not to be absurd, I usually traveled second class. Second class, I assured her, was just fine and all cars were air-conditioned. I told her to stop being such a snob.

"Do as you like," Karen replied calmly, "but we have learned to travel first class in summer and second class in winter. It's not a question of air-conditioning, or status or luxury. It's about deodorant, and I don't mean yours."

Like almost all residents of Provence, Karen and Victor had the framed "before" picture of their house in the dining room. They had taken a run-down century-old *mas,* a country farmhouse, and turned it into a California-style French dream home, cunningly located in the midst of the Côtes du Rhône vineyards. When exchanging addresses with new acquaintances, they commonly said, "Oh, we live in the vines."

Indeed, from the windows all you saw were rows and rows of vines, running from the garden and past the swimming pool to the foothills of the nearest mountain range. The garden was large and magazine-layout worthy—it was Victor's passion. The pool was flanked by two cherry trees, the veranda wrapped around an ancient *tilleul* (linden) tree. We sat out here most evenings for candlelit dinners, enclosed by glass and screens. We listened to the sounds of the fields at night, of frogs and *cigales* (cicadas).

We spent our mornings driving to the various Provençal villages, with plenty of time to visit Isle-sur-Sorgue, the most famous of the flea-market towns. We spent the day touching every *boutis* (bed quilt) in town, comparing prices on Catholic versus Protestant *panetières*—hand-carved wooden cabinets created for storing baguettes of bread. (Catholic is more fancy and therefore more expensive.) While we sat by the pool each afternoon, our feet dangling in the tepid water, we debated whether or not I should buy the green grain bins I had fallen in love with.

Ah, those green bins. They were expensive for what they were: two bureaus consisting of five grain bins each, very dirty and a tad disgusting. The wood had been painted bright green, which I found charming but which brought down the value. Furthermore, the paint was nicked and chipped and jarringly bright. But they talked to me and I wanted them, they screamed of everyone's dreams of rustic French style. That I had no place for them was an almost moot point. They captured the mood of the summer; they were meant to be mine. Somehow, with the greatest of discipline, I left without them. But I began to dream that someday I too would have a country house in France.

58

Karen and Victor invited me to stay for Bastille Day and the local celebrations, which included a family-style dinner in a nearby medieval town, a place that closed its roads to traffic each July 14 in order to place tables in the streets so that anyone could come and picnic and fill up on the locally made wines before dancing until dawn.

But I had already agreed to spend July 14 in Paris with the Tuttles, who were taking me on a picnic, even if it rained. It always rained on July 14. It was an eat-as-you-go picnic rather than the kind carried in a basket. This was the first year of the picnic, which was sponsored by the French government. It was created to get neighbors and strangers to sit down at the table with each other, to talk and share bread and wine. Of course, you sort of chose your neighbors and new friends by what *quartier* you picked. I would have chosen the eighth if I was

alone, but Claire chose Montmartre, so we followed the neighborhood celebrations while we walked uphill, eating as we
went. I had my first ham and butter sandwich. It changed my
life. How had I lived more than fifty years without knowing
about this taste? Funny how the simplest things could have a
major impact on you in France, especially when they touched
your taste buds.

Celebrations actually began before July 14. While reading my
Zurban, one of the guides to weekly events in Paris, I saw information about the traditional firemen's balls, usually held on July
13. I fell in love with the very notion. I tried to remember the
movie I had seen about the firemen's ball, but I just know it was
an art film from my art film days, Milos Forman.

Mike and I had gone to a firemen's ball in L.A. once, although
Mike preferred pancake dinners in small towns. It was a tradition between us, so the idea of going to the ball in Paris made
me giggle. I was looking to meet people, to have new experiences, to become part of France—I figured I should get out
there and see what was going on. Of course, I did have a fashion
panic. What did you wear to a firemen's ball? A Dalmatian coat à
la Cruella De Vil? A slicker? Hose?

Parisian toffs go away for Bastille Day—in fact, most families
take a holiday the day the school holidays begin at the end of
June and stay out of town until July 14 has passed. Firemen's
balls therefore are blue-collar affairs that attract a lot of students
or people who have a keen interest in dancing to loud disco
music and drinking as much as possible. Barfing on the streets at
dawn is optional, but usually part of the drill. The party I chose
seemed lively enough.

Thankfully the music was so loud that no one could talk. This gave me confidence since I wouldn't have to speak French. I merged and mingled and stared for a while, searching for someone older than my son. I think it must have taken me at least a half hour to realize that all the men I was looking at were gay.

Of the dozen or so firemen's balls in Paris, a few are *PD*, as gay is referred to in French. My guidebook had failed to mention this little detail.

59

After a few days back in Paris, spent mostly on the phone flirting with the count and testing new beauty products to rid myself of cellulite, I went off to Bordeaux. Destination: Les Sources de Caudalie, the famous wine spa that is located on the grounds of the Smith Haut-Lafitte vineyard where they practice *vinothérapie,* wine therapy. Yes, wine therapy—cures provided by the properties inside the grape seed and applied to the body. No, you don't drink the wine; you soak in wine by-products and get massaged and pampered with other wine by-products.

Smith Haut-Lafitte is a famous vineyard with a very high rating from Robert Parker (usually in the 90s, depending on the vintage). The vineyard dates back to the time of the Crusades (thus the fleur-de-lys on the shield) but had been bought by Daniel and Florence Cathiard, who, as I understood the story, were ski champions on the French Olympic team, started a chain of sports goods stores, sold them, ended up with buckets of money and bought this vineyard, which was not enjoying its best moments when they took over. Since they were not old Bordeaux aristos, they were actually laughed at when they first came to town in the early '90s. No one was laughing now. In fact, they became the ringleaders of a new gang of vintners and marketing geniuses, ushering in a new regime of marketing and profitability.

The family had just opened the world's first wine spa, a very swank inn that included two restaurants with healthy gourmet food (and two-star chef), wine barrels made into hot tubs and a complete spa center with indoor pool, meditation room and scads of treatment rooms. This is where you got your red wine bath, your Merlot wrap, your wine and honey wrap, the Sauvignon massage, the crushed Cabernet scrub, the anti-aging Vinolift face treatment or the soft peeling with grapes. Peel me a grape, as they say.

I took the TGV to Bordeaux, where a van met me and drove me out of town and toward Martillac, a part of Bordeaux I had not been to before. Normal guests at the spa probably just settle in to zen out or get graped up, but I was immediately invited to the château for a tour and then on to the residence for cocktails with the family because I knew them socially.

Florence and Daniel Cathiard were entertaining another journalist, a Frenchwoman who did not speak English. After the tour of their home, we all sat around the kitchen table and spoke French. Daniel came and went from the room, while Florence kept the conversation going among the women, and translated for me when I got stuck. They invited me to stay for family dinner, but I was working and forced myself to go back to the spa for dinner . . . just another two-star meal in paradise. Florence and I agreed we would get together again in the five days I would be there; Daniel drove me down the big driveway, through the gates and to the spa. I felt as though I had left Tara.

The next day at eight-thirty in the morning, while grapes and honey were being rolled all over my middle-aged body in the first of my scheduled treatments, I received a message to be ready in an hour with my bathing suit and a *casquette* (baseball cap). I had no clothes with me for being kidnapped by the fashionably laid-back of Bordeaux, so I bought a Caudalie T-shirt, pulled on my blue jeans and grabbed my straw hat. There was no explanation from the Cathiards—it was a rather matter-of-fact kidnapping without regard to my anticellulite treatments or need for them.

We drove first to pick up Daniel's mother, who did not speak English, and then we drove to Arcachon to drop *maman* at the house on the beach she was renovating. I learned we had been invited to a picnic on a sandbar so were next headed for the bay and the boat. All conversation was in French, but I got the general idea. They mentioned some friends that would be there and I thought Florence was telling me I would just *love* these people. In fact, I later learned that I mistranslated the French—she said some of the guests were the family that owned Amora mustard. Oops, my mistake.

I was staggered by my reaction to Arcachon, a town I had barely heard of. I could have found it for you on a map of France, but was totally unprepared not only for the powerful effect it would have on me, but the fact that it would throw me back almost fifty years to my childhood summers in Atlantic City. I could not decide if I fell instantly in love with the town because it was at heart like a place I was familiar with (Atlantic City) or if I just have good taste and the fact that both of my grandmothers used to summer in Atlantic City had nothing to do with it. I was conceived in the Traymore Hotel on the boardwalk in the month of July; maybe it was in my blood. I was dumbfounded by the idea that you can arrive in a strange place and immediately feel not only comfortable, but that you belonged there. This was a strange city in a strange country, yet I was not a stranger. Was this a past lives thing? Was the sea in my genes?

My rich grandmother stayed at the Traymore Hotel each summer; my poor grandmother had a cottage right after the end (or beginning) of the boardwalk, a few blocks from the beach. There was a small yard with a million huge, fat, blue-purple hydrangea bushes. It was hardly a villa, yet it was strangely like the villas in Arcachon, each with their names spelled out in tiles across the front—Villa Mimosa, Minnetonka, Maison Azur des Anges, etcetera. People milled around *centre ville* in Arcachon wearing their flip-flops and shorts; the stores were a riot of colored inner tubes, beach pails and butterfly nets. It was a place I already knew and understood and my heart was wild with glee.

Maman's house was the last *maison de grande dame* on the beach, a true *pâtisserie de maison de famille*—a cream puff of a house. From what I grasped of the conversation, it was in terrible shape before she began the work. Now it could qualify as a member of the Leading Hotels of the World chain. It was a small mansion, as mansions go, about four thousand square feet right on the beach. *Maman* was the only woman of her age I ever met who was not downsizing. Or if she was downsizing, she lived in a very large castle, or chalet, in Grenoble, the family seat. *Maman* laughingly rejected the idea of letting me live in the maid's room in order to teach her English.

"But I don't want to learn English," she said somewhat stubbornly.

Ah, I thought to myself, *but I want to live in a mansion in Arcachon.* I spent the train ride back to Paris wondering if I lived in a French mansion by the sea, would I have a place in my life for bright green grain bins from a Provençal flea market.

60

As soon as the weather turned nice, articles on flea markets and how to bargain began to appear in women's magazines. The subject was so popular that magazines were desperate to create a twist to the story each season. One of the home décor magazines had a regular feature on celebrities and their flea market finds; another had a monthly column of before and after shots of finds from the flea markets. Every editor had to skin this cat.

Enter *moi*, hired for my first article for a French magazine. At first I thought they gave me the assignment because of my Born to Shop experience, but it turned out that they really wanted a story about the wife of a famous chef who bought most of the tabletops for her husband's fancy restaurant at the flea market. She had turned them down once, but the editor thought that madame would respond to me. I saw this theme in various business negotiations—Americans were often used as bait or ammunition because of the novelty factor.

I went to dinner at her husband's three-star where she was, in the tradition of most French restaurants, the hostess who worked the room. She wore designer silks and swanned around from table to table, shifting to different languages as she extended her long, thin hand and provided a firm handshake. We met, chatted and I explained who I was and gave her a Born to Shop book. She agreed to the article.

Madame spoke English fluently, of course. She directed me to a specific café in the markets of St. Ouen where I waited (and waited) for her. We sat outside and talked—she drank endless tiny cups of coffee while I sipped a single Coca-Cola. She explained that as far as she was concerned, the markets at St. Ouen were the best, although she also confessed that she worked the Parisian upmarket specialty fairs and sometimes went to Vanves. Then we began our tour. There was no discussion of lunch.

Frankly, I had never really liked the flea markets of St. Ouen at the porte de Clingacourt, a place I call the Big Flea. I knew it well and kept up-to-date for my work, but I rarely went there for fun or to decorate my apartment. I found it not only expensive, but too much of a closed society for an outsider to get a decent deal.

That was the whole point of the story, of course. Madame was an insider and she worked this market every single Sunday, all day. Her philosophy was different from an American's, as was her shopping style. She was not interested in looking at a lot of merchandise since she only bought for the restaurant. She did business with dealers whom she knew and had already bought from—usually over a period of years. If she tried a new shop, it was only after an introduction had been made either by phone prior to her arrival or in person by another dealer. On a Sunday in late July, she taught me her dance—the French ritual of *chiner* (to browse and bargain for *brocante*), which is very different from the way we Americans do it.

When we got to her sources, madame was kissed on each cheek (*bien sûr*), then she introduced me, making it sound as if I was the most famous journalist in America whom she had brought to them as a favor. We were invited to sit, we began the chat in English but quickly switched to French. I invariably dropped out of the conversation and had to pretend that I could follow what was being said. Eventually coffee came, sometimes there was a Coke for me. They talked about business: what's come in and gone out, how the market (as in flea market, not stock market) was moving, where the Americans were and what they were paying since Americans invariably overpaid and were the lifeblood of the business.

Finally, madame asked what new pieces of interest they had. Things then came from the back or from under tables, from the bottom of packed boxes or from shelves that required a footstool or ladder to access. Pieces were touched, some were admired. They talked and talked and talked. It was hard to pretend I was fascinated, or even interested at all, which I knew was what made me American and them French. Americans are direct people; the French like to talk around things. I didn't dare look at my watch. I wanted lunch. I was ready to admit that my approach to shopping was to see as much as possible in as short a time as possible and that frankly, I was bored. While I appreciated the rituals I had been observing from an academic point of view, they didn't really fit my personality. As a generalization, I think American shoppers like to do it and French like to talk about it.

We went to only five dealers that day yet spent more than six hours together. We did not eat lunch; I drank two coffees and two Cokes. Madame had five more coffees (one at each dealer) and many cigarettes. The courtship was done with words and manners; the dealers knew that if madame did not buy that day she would buy another day. They didn't really care, as long as she gave good conversation and played by the rules. Besides, she was famous and her husband had three stars—that counted for a lot in France—and no one was in a hurry. To be in a hurry in France means you are not French.

61

For our first date, the count invited me to dinner at Taillevent. I burst out laughing and refused. "I hate Taillevent and besides, the chef left for the George V," I told him.

"Okay," he snapped impatiently, "then how about Le Cinq?"

Le Cinq is the name of the restaurant at the George V.

It was a divine date, everything it should have been, including low key—if you considered that the dining room had more flowers than the Garden of Eden. Although he would put his hand to the low of my back to guide me into a room, or take my arm to help me at steps, he made no physical moves on me. It was charming . . . and very smart. The count seemed to have great respect for my widowhood or lack of experience. When I was with him, I was not anyone I had ever been in the past fifty-two years of my life, but a new creature altogether. Perhaps Audrey Hepburn; possibly Grace Kelly.

I'd seen him four times during the month, in between our various trips, sometimes for lunches that were extremely proper. Then he invited me to The Ritz for drinks in the late afternoon—something rather odd, I thought.

Aha, I thought to myself, *this is it*.

The Ritz has historically been the place where one observed

what is known as the *cinq à sept* (five to seven), which refers to the hours of the afternoon when gentlemen met their mistresses for drinks and a roll in the hay. This detail was not in *Gigi,* but I learned it from someone or other.

We sat in the garden of The Ritz, sipped cold white wine and, as if conducting a business meeting, the count proceeded to tell me that he enjoyed my company, I made him feel young again and he wanted to pursue a relationship with me.

"What kind of a relationship?" I stuttered.

I mean, who asked permission? Who discussed this sort of thing when a little action went a lot further than a lot of words? Was he going to call my father and ask for my hand in adultery?

"Normal," he said.

I actually burst out laughing. I had never heard of anything more ridiculous in my life. He got a wounded look on his face briefly and then threw back his head and roared with laughter, the folds around his eyes crinkled and his perfect white teeth glistened in the sun. I was ready for him to rip my clothes off me right there in the garden of The Ritz.

"Okay," he said, "I understand, you are American, you are very direct. So what I am trying to say is that I have had some problems. I am not as young as I used to be. I have a little more weight here than I used to. But Viagra works."

The plot thickened.

I had been married for twenty-five years with a reasonably healthy relationship with my husband. I was fifty-two years old. What the hell did I know about Viagra except for what I'd heard from Bob Dole on television ads? The count told me he had booked a room. The pill required an hour and a half before it took effect. Should he take the pill now while we had tea in the garden? Would I like to have dinner? Could I spend the night?

I flashed on Diana and Dodie.

I explained that I hadn't quite planned on this particular moment. I had nothing with me and I cannot sleep without putting medicine in my eyes—I do not keep the medicine in my handbag. Asking him to wait there while I popped into the metro, ran home and got my toothbrush and eye medicine seemed like it could ruin the moment. I did appreciate the romantic notion of doing it for the first time in The Ritz, but I was overtaken with panic. I then remembered the rest of the problem.

"While we're having scientific true confessions, I think you should know that I've never been to bed with anyone who isn't Jewish."

The hearty laughter again. "I will teach you my body," he whispered conspiratorially.

I had never considered a negotiated love affair before, but I had never been widowed or middle-aged before either. We agreed that we would spend the evening together, as he planned it, but I asked him to not take the pill. I just wanted to be held in his arms, to sleep with him and get used to the whole thing. The first step was to keep it simple, to make sure I could handle it.

So to speak.

62

Aside from love affairs and trips to the countryside, the summer was the time for weddings. Many of my French friends were married at the age of twenty-one or twenty-two and became parents shortly thereafter. I arrived in Paris for the weddings of their children as the cycle of early marriages was repeated. By late May, my first invitation had arrived. By July, I was in the thick of the summer wedding season.

My first invitation—the one in May—was an invitation to a wedding, but I was not invited to actually attend it. What I had received in the mail was meant as a wedding announcement, a mere courtesy. It would have been gauche for me to show up. I was not expected to send a gift. The rules were shifty to an American but clear to my French friends.

As further invitations arrived during the summer, it became more clear. When you were truly invited to the wedding, there was not only the invitation itself, but lots of inserts and usually a map, since few of the weddings were held in Paris. The first invite I received was just that, a sole invitation. It was the fact that it had no inserts or response card that alerted me to the fact that I was into a cultural situation I did not understand.

I sought opinions from both Claire and Pascale-Agnès. I learned there were many, many ways of being invited to a wedding in France, each with its own strict protocol. There was a type of invitation wherein you were invited to the wedding Mass and then to a party in order to toast the bride and the groom. After the toasts were given, you knew it was time to leave. Others would have been invited to stay to dinner or for a meal or for more parties, but if your invite read *"vin d'honneur,"* then it was your job to hightail it out of there. A *scandale sociale,* Claire explained to me, was when a guest invited only for the drinks stayed and tried to eat, which of course displaced some of the invited guests. *Quelle horreur!*

How many parts of the wedding you were invited to naturally had to do with your relationship with the family. In France, the religious ceremony was just for show and did not count legally, so before it, a civil ceremony was always performed.

The bride wore a suit and only family attended. Such weddings were most often held in the morning before the religious ceremony or perhaps the day before. They were at the mayor's office or town hall. They were not considered to be a big deal.

The big deal was the part with the white dress and the veil. Usually there was one religious ceremony, but it was not odd for there to be two or more wedding ceremonies—each with a Mass or whatever service was appropriate. Pascale-Agnès had had three weddings, each in different parts of France because members of the groom's family were too old to travel. I think Pascale-Agnès had two different wedding gowns, the second one was for her country wedding in the south of France, which was the last of the three and was a more relaxed event that required a casual wedding gown.

By midsummer, I was invited to a wedding in the southwest. The invitation was issued by the grandmother and the parents of the groom and the parents of the bride. A nice touch, I thought. I did not know any members of the family very well and had never even met the groom (or the bride), so I declined. I was flattered to be invited, but was not going to get involved, especially since I knew that no one in the family spoke English. I wrote a note of regrets in French.

Pascale-Agnès explained that I had to send a gift that cost 30 percent of the expense I would have incurred if I had gone to the wedding. She said this was an ironclad rule. I thought this prospect over for many months and decided that I was an American and therefore allowed to make a social gaffe in French society. The first gift I planned to send was an olive-wood salad set, for fifty dollars. But my Born to Shop nature got the best of me and by summer's end I found horn serving pieces that were chic and stunning and cost twenty dollars. I mean, let's face it, I didn't even know the people involved.

The real wedding of my world was held in the early days of September. The preparations had taken almost two years. Shortly after I arrived in Paris, the parents told me about the wedding and advised me to hold the dates. They also suggested that I buy a suit and hat, which was their way of pointing me in the right fashion direction. Indeed, a French wedding was much like a British wedding in terms of what the guests wore. I think guests at a British wedding tend to wear pastel-colored suits whereas the French wear dress and jacket ensembles—or suits—that are printed with flowers. Many guests look like the living room sofa; when they are mingling around a church or a gathering place, they look like a scene from *Fantasia*.

Because this wedding was in September, it was slightly different from others in that the color palette would change for everyone except the bride. I would need a dark hat, but not a felt hat or real winter hat. A summer suit would not do, but it would be too hot for wool. Flower prints were still appropriate, but not summer flowers. At least I had a shopping problem to keep me occupied that summer.

As I searched for the right suit, I thought maybe I could create a TV game show out of the quest—each week contestants would be sent to the stores and malls of the world to find just the right thing to wear to a special event.

63

In Paris, the summer sales ended by mid-July when fall merchandise arrived. During the summer, the south of France had a totally different sale schedule from the north in order to sell more merchandise at full price to people on vacation. In the United States, the sale merchandise usually stayed on the floor for most of the summer. In Paris, fall fashion was introduced while the temperature outside could well be one hundred degrees. There were actually customers buying fall clothes.

I was among them.

I had learned to do my fall shopping as early as possible in order to find my size. With a wedding to choose clothes for, the anticipation of a romance with the count and my first fall season in Paris approaching, I couldn't wait to get to the fall merchandise. For my real life before I moved to France, I rarely paid regular retail price. It was against my personal principles. France has fewer chances for bargain shoppers and much less selection than the United States. I would have to pay top euro.

On top of that, I am a large size by French standards, a 46. Stores got much more stock in sizes 38 and 40, but few pieces in the larger sizes. In fact, they might have only one size 46 and when it was gone, it was gone. There was no stock in the back; another piece would not arrive to fill in from a distribution center that was in touch with a computer that told the store to restock. Department stores or branches of a multiple would not call another store to locate the piece you wanted in the size you needed, even if they could track it on the computer.

Although a size 46 is not really the equivalent of an American 16 (it's closer to a 14), like the size 16 in the United States, it is the end of the line. Most French lines did not make a larger size, you had to buy from the plus-size brands or the Italians. (Thankfully Armani goes up to size 52.) But I wanted to wear a French brand to the wedding. I decided to go to Chanel, where whatever I bought would be considered an investment and while I did not have several thousand dollars to blow on a suit, I thought maybe I could buy a jacket or a piece that would go with what I already owned.

"Do you have this in a size forty-six or forty-eight?" I asked the saleswoman, as I fingered a woven raw silk tweedy jacket.

Her eyes grew wide and she truly gasped aloud.

"*Mon dieu, madame!*" she murmured, too horrified to hide her reaction.

I faxed my tailor in Hong Kong.

64

When I told friends I was moving to Paris, they were skeptical about my social life. If they didn't come out with that old story about the French being rude, they lectured me on what a closed society it was and that few real French people would welcome me or even be nice to me. They said I would never be invited into a Parisian's home or make real French friends. They were wrong.

I have never found the French rude. In fact, the rudest thing I heard from anyone came from an American journalist I bumped into the first week I lived in Paris. She said it was hard enough to get work as a freelancer and she resented my arrival because I would take work from her and everyone else. Now that's rude.

By the time I had lived in my building for six months, most of the residents knew me and said hello. Some even stopped for a few words. It was always a few words, since I didn't know too many more. I knew the shopkeepers who had storefronts in the building by name, the concierge was almost nice to me, my next-door neighbors asked to borrow not a cup of sugar but a *friteuse* (a special pot for making French fries) and my upstairs neighbor, Dominique, was becoming a real friend. But then, she was my age, spoke English perfectly and had lived in America for ten years.

Dominique was actually friendly from the minute I moved in; I think the others had a wait-and-see attitude. They warmed up and acknowledged me at six months; they began to accept me after a year. I had no doubt that in a few years' time I would be considered part of the team.

In the first few days of my residence, Dominique stopped me in the courtyard and said to me in French that she noticed I had arrived and she wanted to introduce herself. As soon as I responded to her in French, she switched to English. I met her husband, her daughter, her dog. By the summer, she invited me up to see her apartment, which was directly above mine. She thought this might be of interest to me since she had the exact same space. She owned her apartment and I rented mine, but I was curious to see how the identical space could be used differently.

Despite all the decorator magazines I have read in my life, I was shocked at the difference in Dominique's apartment from mine. I had never done major renovations or construction on any of my homes, so I didn't have that much experience or vision when it came to moving walls or re-creating space. My apartment was a railroad flat, with a very, very long corridor and boring rooms that jutted off it. Dominique's apartment was a miracle of sun and light . . . with squarer rooms and much less hallway.

She had a full—and large—bathroom where my dining room was. She had taken down the entry wall, which eliminated the front portion of the long hallway and made her living room almost square. Because our kitchens were enormous (I actually had a sofa bed in mine), she had created an eat-in kitchen with a large Provençal dining table and eight chairs. She had eliminated all the pipes and water tanks that I was forced to live with, but had not torn out the chimney to the stove—which she confessed my apartment once had. She was stuck with the rest of the long hallway, but she had put built-in cabinetry from floor to ceiling, so she was using the space well and added charm by using a good cabinetmaker who embellished his work with nice trim and a rustic, country style.

In the space where I had my bathroom, Dominique had a *dressing*—hers was a laundry room as well as a walk-in closet. She and her husband had chosen the same bedroom that I used for myself; their daughter still lived at home and had the larger bedroom. In order to gain space, she had eliminated two of the apartment's three fireplaces, which was a decision that I could never have made no matter how much space could be gained.

Dominique and I had a relationship like most neighbors— maybe not like Lucy and Ethel, but she accepted packages for me or helped me with some translations when I couldn't understand the French. We had never done anything socially until one day she knocked on my door and announced that she was inviting me, I had to go with her right away. I was wearing shorts and a T-shirt. No problem, she promised.

After we walked two blocks I couldn't stand the suspense any more. I have always hated surprises. "Where are we going?" I demanded.

"Don't you read the papers?" she asked. "Don't you know that they have just announced the winner of the Baguette of the Year . . . and that the baker's shop is around the corner from us, right here in the seventeenth?"

On a hot day in July, my neighbor and I were out for a stroll to test the best bread in Paris. We discussed bread as we walked: chewy, doughy, yeasty, crunchy; Poilane versus Poujauran—two of Paris's most famous *boulangers*. We wondered aloud if Lionel Poilane's tragic death would change the quality of the product. We chatted and stood in line in the sun, waiting for our chance to buy La Baguette Rétrodor, not only the winner of the contest but a bread with a registered name, its own specialty paper wrapping and Web site, www.retrodor.com.

It's no secret that the French take their bread seriously. Every first-time tourist knows to only buy bread at shops that have long lines. We talked about the mass-market chain Paul, from Lille, and whether or not they had sold out and gotten too commercial or still offered a valuable product. It was what passed for intellectual discussion in Paris in summer.

When it was our turn, Dominique asked me how I liked my bread cooked, as if we were discussing eggs or lamb. I happen to like it rare, but I didn't know anyone cared. When it was our turn, she ordered three breads—one not well cooked for me, one very well cooked for her and one regular to bring back to our concierge. Aha, I thought to myself, the way to the concierge's heart was through her taste buds.

65

It was a good time to finally get in with the concierge, because the houseguests began to arrive in force; many of them needed to get the keys from her. Houseguests had been arriving since I moved to Paris, first Aaron and then friends of the family. Some people chose to express their condolences by coming to Paris and staying with me, helping to cheer me up through the first winter and into spring.

By summer, the guests were frequently those who preferred not to pay for a hotel room. I invited some of them; others invited themselves. My favorites were the kids of my peers, or friends of my son, who I knew were delighted to have a place to bunk in and who I knew were much nicer to me than they would have been if I didn't have an apartment in Paris. I got to practice mothering; they got a free place to stay and a little home cooking. It was a win-win, as they say.

A few of my houseguests were people who might not have been able to come to Paris if they didn't have someplace to stay. Peter Greenberg, one of my oldest friends and a fellow travel writer (and a travel TV personality), sent me his housekeeper and her daughter. On their first day in the apartment, I took out a map of Paris, drew a circle around my apartment's location and then pointed to the Arc de Triomphe, a few blocks away.

"We are three blocks from the Arc de Triomphe," I explained, as I pointed with the marker along the route on the map.

They stared at me blankly. They looked down at the map.

They looked out to the courtyard. I soon learned they had not read any guidebooks, knew nothing of Paris and had never heard of the Arc de Triomphe.

"Okay," I said to them, "what have you heard of that we can use as a landmark?"

"Princess Diana," they chorused. "We want to see where Princess Diana died. Is that near you?"

66

Before the count returned to Paris, when I expected he would spend a few nights at my apartment instead of in his usual hotel, I decided to spruce things up a bit. I wanted to make sure my apartment was as elegant as possible. I guess part of my definition of elegant is clean.

I am not by nature a neat person. I think people who have clean houses have no imagination. But for the sake of my love affair, I was ready to surrender some of my creativity.

And so I met Calvin Klein, my new houseman. I found him from another American expat who used him once a week, who got him from a French person who used him three times a week and swore he was not only fantastic but able to do more than clean: he cooked, he catered meals, he served dinner parties, he dog-sat, he ran errands.

There was no dispute about his real name; none of us knew it. He arrived at each job wearing a Calvin Klein T-shirt, said his name, which was complicated in an Asian way where first and last names were backward and forward and therefore confusing, so he was named Calvin Klein on the spot and nick-named CK.

CK said he spoke English, but that couldn't be particularly well proven. As far as I could tell, he didn't speak too much English or French . . . and only pretended he understood what was being said. I recognized the problem because I've done it myself with the same bad results.

In the beginning, CK did a fabulous job cleaning and since his price was right (eight dollars an hour), I had him two days a week for three hours each. As time passed, however, I realized that he seldom did good work but he was miraculously efficient on the day before I vowed to fire him, so he stayed on. I was also impressed with his honesty. Honesty was next to godliness in my book; cleanliness came later.

Besides, cleaning the house myself was not very satisfying, partly because as I said I'm not too neat to begin with and partly because I didn't like the products I was using and could not get them to perform well. After three hours of cleaning my house, I never felt as if I had accomplished anything. It didn't have that sparkling feel, that "inhale deeply and smell the clean" feel.

I could not achieve that smell in France because here, the products all come with sweet scents—the one called Normandie, which I had unfortunately invested heavily in, was a fake apple smell that could make a sensitive person puke. Choices in cleaning products were usually lavender, apple, spring flowers or lemon-orange. To an American, clean means a chemical smell. In my childhood, I liked the smell the school floors had after they were scrubbed by the janitor; I hated the smell of fake apples. Furthermore, it offended me to think that a toilet bowl was meant to smell like a fruit bowl.

CK was equally disenchanted with my selection of products. He sent me out on a whole new shopping spree so that I might have a properly stocked French via the Philippines utility closet. I was to buy: Javel products (with amonia) for cleaning; Vitres for window washing; Cif for cleaning the sink and Cedar floor wax . . . and no other brands. He didn't approve of my powdered Ajax (the foaming cleanser, *ba ba ba boom*) simply because he had never seen it before. Now Ajax is popular in France, but then it was unknown and therefore could not be trusted.

I imported large quantities of spray starch from the United States, a product that I have never found on the shelves in France. Normal French people ironed with a spray called *eau de repasssage* (ironing water) or *eau glissé,* which translates as smooth water. Then they invented scented ironing water, which became a fashion statement and de rigueur in the aristocrat's home.

Despite the variety of fancy, scented waters now on the shelves in France, the warnings on my iron said not to use them, so I stayed with Niagara, which CK went through at such a clip that I was certain he was selling it on the streets. Maybe he thought it was Viagra.

Having a houseman made a difference in my social chitchat. Then I learned that having a houseman who was paid money was very *déclassé*. Most of my friends who have staff have worked out trade deals—they let some illegal immigrant live in their *chambre de bonne* for free in exchange for X number of hours of house cleaning and party service. The ultimate was to lend out your help to a needy friend who was giving a soiree. You did this with the same largesse that perhaps Louis B. Mayer used when lending out Clark Gable.

67

Friends from New York came to Paris on business in the last week of August, proving that someone, somewhere, thought there was business to be done in France in August. I had only a few days' notice before they arrived, but was nonetheless called upon to suggest the newest places to eat and to make the reservations for a luncheon together. Since it was August, I felt we would be able to get a table at any of the restaurants on the hit—or "it"—list I kept on my desk, which listed all the newest choices to be tested.

I chose one of the newest Costes brothers' creations.

The Costes brothers took Paris by the stilettos a few years ago when they opened places like Café Beaubourg across from the Centre Pompidou and Café Marly in the Louvre. Then came the Costes Hotel and a string of other cafés, until finally they seemed to have taken over Paris. In the year that I had been there, baby Costes's had popped up all over and it was important for one's social status to have visited, tasted and tested.

I called the chosen restaurant and explained whom I was entertaining—an important international publishing executive— and that I only wanted to make a reservation if we could be guaranteed excellent seating and a fine appreciation for our pedigrees. No problem, madame.

I got to the restaurant a few minutes early. I was as chic as any model in *Vogue,* dressed in a mélange of prints in burnt orange, raspberry and cranberry that straddled the summer-fall crest in a town where you don't wear white shoes after *Assomption* (August 15). I had on designer shoes and carried an expensive handbag. My eyes were lined in kohl and lacquered with two layers of mascara. I was dressed for lunch in Paris, or anywhere in the world where the guests had, as Scott Fitzgerald put it, a laugh like money . . . the newest Gucci bag . . . and a pair of Tods in the closet.

I was shown to a table under, I don't mean next to, I mean directly *under* the stairwell. So much for my designer duds. I said it wouldn't do. I was taken to a table upstairs. I asked for the manager.

Like most restaurants in Paris, this one clearly had A and B parts as well as even less desirable locations where hangers-on were happy to be seated in order to observe the scene . . . or be able to tell the friends back home where they dined, leaving out the detail about being seated next to the kitchen door.

The manager seemed unimpressed with me, my linguistic skills and my Dries Van Noten outfit. I gave him one of my business cards from Galeries Lafayette—where I had been a consultant for two years—and wrote down the name of my friends and in large letters, under which I wrote Hachette, the name of the largest publishing company in France.

I sipped a Coke and fumed . . . even in the *non-fumez* area.

A few minutes later I saw my friend Jean-Louis heading toward me from the toilets. "Ah, there you are," he said between kisses. "We were waiting for you downstairs."

Astonished, I went downstairs, where Barbara and Jean-Louis had been installed at one of the best tables in the house. No one had thought to tell me of the change in venue. And no one ever told me what had been the magic word that turned us into superstars: it might have been the brand names—Galeries Lafayette or Hachette, but I don't know. In many ways, it didn't matter. I learned that it's not how you're dressed but the old standard who you know.

68

August was ghostlike in its emptiness and zombielike in its mental vacancy. Paris ceased to be part of the rest of France. Parisians who stayed in town were in almost total denial as to the existence of a real world. August was a ballet in slow motion, performed on an empty stage by the second string, those smart enough to visit when the city was deserted or those too poor to have a summer home or place to hide out. Few businesses considered staying open in order to rake in the big bucks. No stores had promotions on sheets, which would have been handy since all the laundries were closed. I bought two new sets of sheets at outrageous French prices.

In August, you could go to a hit movie on the Champs Elysées and not have to wait in line. (Movie theaters were air-conditioned too.) You could get into dinner without a reservation, provided of course, that your restaurants of choice were even open. You could get parking on the street and it was free, in both July and August. You could stroll anywhere and have the luxury of space.

Of course, there were a few problems to cope with. The dry cleaner, where I inadvertently left a large pile of summer clothes, closed toward the end of July while I was out of town and did not reopen until the end of August. Likewise, the manicure salon and my hair salon closed up, without so much as a postcard or sign out front directing you to an on-duty source. By law, the pharmacy had to post the nearest open pharmacist whenever it closed. The woman who did my hair color should have been required to do the same. Roots rerouting, or something.

It was so dull that I decided to go to London, partly because I hadn't been there in ages, partly because my hair color and condition were a disaster that the French didn't seem able to solve. Knowing that the count and I would spend some time together at the end of the month gave me the impetus to get serious about my beauty routine. I needed a trip to Michaeljohn, the salon I had used regularly in Beverly Hills when I lived there and in London when I was in town doing research. These were the guys who made Princess Anne beautiful; obviously they could do anything.

I have long thought that London is to Paris what San Francisco is to L.A. (or vice versa). When we moved to Los Angeles, I swore I would go to San Francisco once a month "to save my sanity." As it turned out, I loved L.A. and went to San Francisco maybe a total of four times in ten years. I really wanted to go to London three or four times a year now that I was settled in Paris. It was time to begin the new habit.

I booked my regular room at The Dorchester at a summer rate. I may have been the only guest at The Dorchester who traveled second class on Eurostar, but I didn't care. The finest linen sheets in the world were soon beneath my feet and I was again amazed—as I was each time I made the trip—at the enormous difference between London and Paris. This was my first trip as a French resident; my needs were slightly different from my American days. Mostly, I wanted to load up on books in English, since they are very expensive in Paris. I spent an hour each day in Hatchards, my favorite London bookstore, and shipped home scads of books.

My reading tastes had changed in the months since Mike had died. I had begun to read his books after he died as it made me feel connected to him. They were far more highbrow than my own. I found a new taste for alternating literature with trash. I didn't quit James Patterson and Jilly Cooper but I also bought novels based on their whimsical titles or cover art, by the prizes they had won, by the buzz they had created among my friends or reviewers. When I bought the British newspapers each Sunday in Paris, I clipped out reviews and bought the books in London. When I found an author I liked (Anita Shreve, Philippa Gregory, Jeffrey Deaver), I bought the collected works, or whatever was on the shelves.

I now read a lot more fiction than I had in my old life. Since I didn't understand what was aired on television very well, I needed more books for pure entertainment. It was also a delicious feeling to throw books into a basket and say, "Ship these to my home in Paris, please." Amazon.com was great, but this was more heady stuff.

Michaeljohn is only one block from Hatchards. Although I had not been to the salon in about four years, when I stepped through the door I felt oddly at home. Kate, who did my hair in London, wasn't there and no one knew me, but I saw other women who looked the way I wanted to look and I felt a connection to them that I had never shared with Frenchwomen. It was elegant and casual all at the same time. My assorted trips to Carita in Paris were fine for a woman of independent means but far too expensive for regular real life. The brand-name salons I subsequently tried were a dance with the devil. Once inside Michaeljohn, I knew I'd never have *I Love Lucy* hair again.

As it turned out, a hefty percentage of the color customers at Michaeljohn come over from Paris—it's a well-known secret that, despite what fashion magazines would have you think, sophisticated hair coloring is not a French specialty. I left with hair that had been spun into three different shades of copper and gold. My new look was Hollywood without being theatrical; it was French without being John Galliano. I have long thought that hair color is the most important cosmetic a woman has; this trip was the proof that it took a continent to make a woman.

I skipped out the door with the recipe tucked into my passport and enough color to last for two months' worth of touch-ups. I agreed that every three months I would come to London for the streaks, which were the effect that made the color so sensational. I had a few seconds of fear that I was tying myself to an unreasonable number of trips to London, but then relaxed—Paris to London was no big deal. Furthermore, I finally knew what the politicos meant when they talked about a united states of Europe and of citizens who were Europeans. When I tossed my hair in the dull light of another overcast London day, I knew that I had become part of the whole. I was Global Woman.

69

When I realized that I needed a fax machine (so the count and I could send mash notes to each other), I bought a very expensive Sharp model, top of the line, for about $500. I also bought an additional three-year warranty that cost another $150.

When it came to electronics in France, we were never talking about small investments, but you convinced yourself to spend the money because you thought that you got what you paid for. I used to think the French were brand conscious because they were snobs. It took only a few weeks of living in France to learn that so many things break and fall apart in France that the public prefers brand names with the hope that manufacturers will stand behind their products.

When I bought this machine and took it home and gave it love and shelter, I could not know that it was loaded with killer bees or that chocolate sauce would have made a better imprint than what the French call the *cartouche* (cartridge.) I had not yet realized that many companies, which have spent millions or billions of dollars to establish their brands on an international basis, will do anything to get into a marketplace. In order to offer their product at a competitive local price, they will cut corners or make cheap versions of their real item, seeking to trade on their famous name and investment in establishing their brand worldwide. It didn't take me long to decide that most brand-name products were no better than the no-name products and that if they were made in France, they all sucked.

When the fax machine broke down, about three weeks after buying it, I calmly walked it back to Darty, where I had made the purchase. Thankfully, there was a branch of Darty (an appliance supermarket) not far from my home; in retrospect, I should have rented an apartment across the street . . . or saved on rent and just slept on the Darty floors.

I had already had a wonderful experience with Darty when my new French television had broken. Darty prides itself on customer service, a concept most French businesses have never considered or understood. Because the first problem had been so easily solved, I thought this was going to be a breeze.

Now then, before I go any further, I want to remind you of

the mimeograph machine, what we used in the dark ages before photocopying was invented or made inexpensive enough for mass use. The mimeograph machine, which was owned by businesses not individuals, worked on a drum system. Ink went inside the drum; the page to be reproduced went on the outside surface of the drum. You used a hand crank to turn the drum; each turn created an imprint. Obviously the drum worked in reverse so you had to check your work by reading backward.

Okay, so every single fax machine in France works on the same old-fashioned drum system. There are no cartridges like we use in the civilized world, but long rolls of inked carbon paper stuff that must be threaded around the drum and into the fax machine so that you can receive faxes.

My godson Jean-Philippe, by then age fifteen, set up the fax machine for me when I bought it. I can't stand to call him every time something ceases to function. So when the fax machine stopped working, I took it back to Darty where they informed me that it wasn't broken, it simply needed a new *cartouche*. I had never read the manual (after all, it was in French) or seen the inside of the machine, so I was in for a rude shock.

Knowing that I am dumb in this department, and already at Darty anyway, I bought six boxes of carbon rolls and asked the man at the service desk to install a new one for me. I was quite surprised to see that I was essentially buying rolls of carbon paper, but I didn't think that much about it, I was too busy congratulating myself on being smart enough to have found someone to help me, and for free. *Every time I need a new cartouche, I'll just come over here,* I thought smugly.

The serviceman had great difficulty putting in the new *cartouche*. I remembered that Jean-Philippe had said it was a bitch of a job. Several Japanese salesmen were consulted while I looked on and tried to flutter my eyelashes helplessly. I kissed the serviceman on the cheeks to thank him when the job was completed. *(Voilà, madame.)* I again congratulated myself on my smart thinking and confidently took the fax home.

I plugged it in and tested it. It worked, but with one small problem: everything printed on the page came out backward. Obviously the roll had been inserted the wrong way.

I went back to Darty. First the serviceman accused me of changing the ribbon when I got home and putting it in backward after he had done it right. Then he passed me to a different person, saying he couldn't work with someone like me. I was furious. Each of the new clerks tried to change the ribbon or insert a new one, without luck. The ribbons cost about twenty dollars each; they were using up my ribbons without so much as a *merci beaucoup*. I spent two hours there. Finally, I asked for a new machine.

I was told that I couldn't have a new machine because ten days had passed since I had bought this machine. I was only entitled to free repairs because I had a warranty. Okay, I said, fix it. But it wasn't broken, they told me.

The machine again passed around from one "expert" to another. I waited longer and fumed more. At one point I was told—with a certain regard that I can only categorize as French—that the machine was finally fixed. *Voilà, madame!*

Yeah? Then what was that piece doing out of the machine and sitting on the counter?

The manager took over. I waited another hour. (I had now been there more than three hours.) He then calmly announced that the machine had been sent back to Sharp to be repaired.

"But it's not broken," I said.

"It is now," he sighed.

I had an instant vision of someone in the back room getting frustrated and taking a hammer to the fax machine, just so it could be broken and then officially sent out to Sharp. Voilà, madame; *smack, crack.*

The fax machine happened to also be my main telephone and most important, my only answering machine. I was told the machine would be ready in ten working days, which was basically more than two weeks in real time, because there was a French holiday in there.

"How will I last for two weeks without an answering machine?" I demanded of the woman at the cash register.

"It's August," she said to me with a shrug. "Who would call you in August?"

70

With more of August on my hands and no French country house, I decided to go to Texas to see my family. After all, there was an expat tradition of going Stateside in August. And besides, my niece Julia always spent some of August in Texas and it was a small tradition that I see her then. It is terribly hot in Texas in August, but unlike Paris, they have air-conditioning. I bought a cheapie ticket online and began to dream about the Delicious Tamale Factory.

I grew up in San Antonio; it has long been my touchstone for real life in America. When I lived in the United States, I visited once a year. Now I thought about Texas a lot because I wondered if I moved back to the United States, where would I live? If Paris had been simply an experiment, it was soon going to be time to decide what to really do with the rest of my life.

I wanted to use the Texas visit as more than a family social call and opportunity to pig out on Tex-Mex. I needed to create my own comparison study of San Antonio and Paris. Not that these two cities had many superficial similarities, but the cost of living in each was more or less the same. Before I totally gave my heart to France or sold my house in New England, I wanted a chance to compare the lifestyles and the prices, to analyze the social situation and see how many trips to Super Target and Costco I would enjoy making in one day.

Item	Paris	New York	San Antonio
Rent: 1,000-square-foot apartment, nice area	$2,000 month	$3,500 month and up	$1,100 month
Unlimited use, AOL	$15	$24.99	$24.99
Ingredients for home-cooked dinner for two, chicken/no wine	$10	$16	$14
Parking overnight in garage	$17	$30	Huh?
Bus or metro ticket	$1.25	$1.50	Who takes a bus?
Manicure	$50 a month with fills	$100 month/fills & glue alternate weeks	$85 month/fills & glue alternate weeks
Household help	$8 an hour	$60 an hour	$25 an hour
Doctor's visit	$35	$300	$150

All in all Texas seemed appealing, but there were a few drawbacks to consider. I was allergic to live oak trees, for one. Sometimes my father made me feel like I was still thirteen years old. Being there made me painfully aware that my mother and my sister were dead—and buried—in San Antonio. As laid-back and comfy as it was to be there, I didn't get any sense of the energy that electrifies the air in cities like New York, Boston, London or Paris. On the other hand, maybe by definition home should be low-key and travel should be exhilarating. Maybe I was being greedy—I wanted chocolate ice cream every day. Living in Texas meant having tortillas every day.

There was also the question of social circles. I had only a handful of friends left over from my youth. Yet with my father's remarriage, I inherited a whole new family and would have many family obligations if I moved to San Antonio . . . obligations mostly to people I was related to only through marriage. Certainly all the holidays would be spent with this group of people, with finding my place at their table and doing things their way. Moving back to Texas would mean being a soldier in my stepmother's army. There was comfort in all this, but no adventure.

San Antonio was a great place to grow up and I would always remember the Alamo, but I reluctantly decided that I didn't want to live in Texas and travel to France. I wanted to live in France and travel the world.

I put my house in Connecticut up for sale.

71

Even though a large percentage of Americans who lived in Paris went to the United States at some point in the summer, it was still polite to ask your friends if they needed any items that you could bring back for them. I got into the habit of springing for the price of an extra piece of checked baggage on the way back to France so I could do what I did best: shop.

Each trip had a somewhat different theme, depending on my needs back in Paris, but I always loaded up on foodstuffs that you couldn't easily get in France and on simple requests from friends. Here is what I bought and what I brought back for others; clearly American food did not have the gourmet reputation attached to French food, but we all missed it nonetheless.

For myself:
Bath towels, $4.99 each at TJ Maxx
Bath sheets, $6.99 each
Two packages Kraft Singles
Two tubes Pillsbury Grands, buttermilk
Four packages Philadelphia cream cheese
One jar maraschino cherries
One large bag shelled pecans
Three tubes Close-Up red gel toothpaste
Four dozen homemade tamales from Delicious Tamale
    Factory

For Dinny:
Package of microwave popcorn, light

For Sherry:
    Two large boxes of Cheerios
    Two packages of Wick Fowler Chili mix

For Andy:
    Cheddar cheese, sharp

72

I met my son and his friend Amanda ("She's a girl and she's a friend but she's not my girlfriend, Mom") back in Paris. As August was coming to a close, we had a need to be Parisian-style August do-nothing-bums while getting over jet lag, to maximize the social acceptability of doing nothing. Then we took the train to Biarritz and holed up in a large room in the Hôtel du Palais, one of my dream hotels. It was indeed a palace once, built by Napoléon III for his wife, Eugénie, who was Spanish and wanted a view of the sea and Spain. Amanda had become so much a part of the family that the three of us shared a room. We had long ago worked out our system, so days were spent independently, then I took them out to dinner. Then they went to clubs; I went to bed.

We decided to share a day hike across the hills above the ocean landscape, and were enjoying the view when my portable phone rang. It was the real estate broker from Westport to announce the house was sold. In fact, it didn't really go on the market. The bid came in during the broker's open house. I didn't get quite as much money as I wanted, but was happy it was over in a day and to know I didn't have to waste any more money on upkeep.

I knew Aaron was upset, but I was upset too. Even more than Mike's funeral, the sale of our family home was a reminder that life would never be the same, that we had suffered enormous losses, that Thomas Wolfe was right, we couldn't go home again. In fact, Aaron came out of it feeling that he didn't have a home at all while at least I had Paris. Aaron felt cheated. I felt empty and guilty and confused. Yeah, I had just gotten rid of that pesky U.S. cable television bill, but had I done the right thing?

73

Before I could answer adequately that question, it was time to prepare for my end of summer rendezvous with the count. I was desperate to accomplish home improvements and personal improvements before our time together. I needed a Brazilian wax. In fact, I became fascinated with the atavistic impulse I could only call sexual preening. Beauty night—a ritual I performed as a single woman in college and in Manhattan before I was married— was something I hardly ever thought about until the imminent arrival of the count. Then I was eighteen all over again.

I read magazines for the latest treatments and products. I prowled the shelves of pharmacies, dime stores and *hypermarchés* looking for French products that guaranteed instant results (they all did). I entered into a sexually aware plateau that created some sort of constant buzz; I probably glowed in the dark.

It seems to me an American notion that when a special event

is coming up, you go into overdrive and work for fast results. Frenchwomen work their regime from the other side of the philosophy—it is a must-do, a part of the life cycle, not a special ritual but a regular experience. Every mother teaches her daughter to go to the esthetician at the onset of puberty.

For those who have little money, there are places like Yves Rocher—a mass market purveyor of beauty treatment. The high-end names were more known for a style or a type of cure. I discovered Anne Semonin years ago, when she was just a cult heroine making nice-smelling goops with essential oils. Her jet-lag treatment actually seemed to work. Now she is internationally famous with salons all over Paris, one in London and one in New York. I no longer had jet lag but I wanted to be made more French than Pamela Harriman to be ready for the count. I turned myself in to be wrapped in seaweed and Saran Wrap, slathered in warm oils and swabbed with serenity. The French believed many things that American women were skeptical about:

- that these things really made a difference;
- that consistent and regular practice made perfect;
- that *bien-être* (well-being) was a side-effect of these treatments and affected a person's overall health.

The only theme I could swallow was the *bien-être* notion. Since moving to France I had accepted the good life and felt better for it. Did the good life come from a jar or a lifestyle? That was the real question. Did it smell like lavender and honey or come with slowing down, taking time to smell the lavender and the honey? Did it really matter if I slathered on the Aroma Calm or not? Did any of these things do a bit of good?

Oh yes, *bien sûr,* said my friends—even Claire. They encouraged me to sign up for more and more cures. And then told me about the ultimate beauty treatment I should try before my rendezvous with the Count of Monte Cristo: a trip to the gynecological osteopath. While French physical therapists provide treatment for women who have recently given birth, the gynecological osteopath is used by women with sexual disorders or by those who need to tighten the vaginal muscles and learn a few tricks.

I couldn't go. Somewhere I could hear my husband's ghost laughing his ass off.

74

The improvements did not end with my body. I had now lived in my apartment six months. It was almost finished, but not quite. I did not have curtains on the windows, partly because I had been loath to spend the money when I didn't know if I was staying longer than one year. With my house sold, and the idea of staying in Paris, I headed to Montmartre and the marché St. Pierre, the discount fabric district.

This is not the Montmartre of the movie about the gamin Amélie, this is the one populated by bargain hunters who rifle through bins in the street at various odd-lot jobbers, who watch their handbags while they cozy up to remnants in the hopes of finding a couture cut-off or a designer rip-off.

A trip to this part of Paris was as good as a trip to Disneyland Paris for me. I emerged into a tri-level metro station as jammed as Grand Central Station at 5:13 P.M. I pushed my way to the street and began the slow climb up the hill toward the church.

Tourists were going to the church, wannabe interior designers and fashion victims were headed to the jobbers who lined the rue Steinkerque. I had been here many times before, but always for clothes—never for fabrics or home décor.

I worked the two-square-block area from door to door until I was almost blind with choices and possibilities. I would have preferred to think it over and return another time, but I had a lot to do before the count came calling, so I chose gauzy yellow see-through chiffony stuff for the guest room, where I expected to sleep with the count, and more formal fabrics for the living room, where the seduction would occur. Along with the fabrics, there were meters of trims in coordinating shades and big tie-backs with heavy tassels. They cost a lot and weighed even more. No wonder there was a French Revolution.

It took me several days to arrange the draperies. The sewing machine had never worked and the idea of doing all those hems and seams was depressing anyway. In the end, I mounted my fourteen-foot ladder with fabric under my arm and scissors in hand. Once firmly perched above my world, I sliced into the fabric and made a series of ties so that the fabrics could be tied right onto the curtain rods. I merely turned the raw edges of the selvages under at the floor, so no hem was required. Then I looped more fabric up and around into the tassels that tied back part of my instant drapes and stood back to admire my work. *Voilà*—the rooms were now finished and sufficiently Frenchified.

75

After all that time and money spent on getting the apartment camera ready, or count ready, the count did not even come to my apartment. He invited me over to the Hotel Meurice to spend a few days. I was to be his sort of live-in honey after all.

The Case of the Curious Circumcision turned out to be no big deal. So to speak. At first, I couldn't even tell the difference and felt like a real idiot. Then the count revealed the Secret of the Sliding Sides and I learned a new *truc* (trick, knack). The count said practice made perfect. *Et voilà.*

I think that once you have been married or are used to living with someone, it's easier to adjust to living with someone else quickly. I was used to there being someone else in the room; someone on the other side of the bed reading the newspaper. Someone else who snored or farted or swore or zapped through all the television stations. Because we had spent so much time on the phone and were so comfortable together, the sexual obstacles seemed less problematic. We laughed a lot. When he told me, in French, that I had the most beautiful breasts in the world, I sighed.

I was crazy about him and crazy in love with the idea of being in love and the thought that I was attractive, that someone wanted me, that at fifty-two I was still sexy. Living in his suite in the Meurice made me giddy. It wasn't just the sex—it was the ritual of having a boyfriend, a lover. There is something far more powerful than alcohol in the notion that an attractive and desirable man wants you. I had almost forgotten what this felt like. Desire is its own aphrodisiac.

We went out to dinner every night. I gave up my rich hippie dress for the Comtesse de Monte Cristo look—a tailored suit with a silk shell, pearls and an important-looking brooch. Of course, I don't own any important jewelry at all, but I do know where the fake stuff is sold. I remembered Queen Elizabeth II's coronation—the first thing I ever saw on television—and my decision at that time to grow up to be a princess. Being a faux countess wasn't so far off.

We ate a lot of our meals at the Meurice since the count was often too tired at the end of a day to play "where should we eat" (one of my best games). We soon had two regular haunts: the Meurice and Davé. Davé, for the uninitiated, is a Chinese restaurant that is constantly written up in *Women's Wear Daily,* which is where I learned about it. To the naked eye, it may appear to be just another Chinese restaurant. In fact, Davé is a private club for the fashion and retail industries and for those in the know. Davé himself must know you, welcome you and kiss you on both cheeks. When Davé began to *tutoyer* me, to use the familiar version of French verbs, a treat reserved for family and close friends, I knew I had made it in Parisian society. Most diners are regulars and because this is one of the few restaurants that is open on Sunday nights, there are a lot of Sunday night regulars who have come to know each other across the tables.

Abby—one of my buddies from Les Girls—and her husband are regulars; they are the ones who brought me into the club. The count and I had dinner with them one night, and though the count has access to every place in France because of his title and pedigree, he too was charmed by Davé. We went there every Sunday night of the *rentrée* season when the count was in Paris. Years ago I had read about Davé and dreamed I would be part of that world. Then, without even trying, I was.

 *Fall*

Chez Francis, place d'Alma, 8e
Pour boire: noisette

The fall season demanded a change in lifestyle and a change in cafés. I decided to add weight training to my exercise program and began to go to the gym at the Hotel Plaza Athénée, about ten minutes from my apartment via the number 92 bus. My worst time of the day was about four P.M., so I figured that was the perfect time to get out of the house and force myself to tighten my abs and find my derrière du fer.

    Chez Francis, a bistro made famous because of its direct view of the Eiffel Tower, was between the bus stop and the Plaza, as we called the Plaza Athénée. Mike and I had been regulars for years; we had even celebrated some of our New Year's Eves there. Chez Francis was still one of my favorite places in Paris, because of the view and the sense that you owned Paris. Though it had memories of my husband, it did not make me sad. Instead, I smugly sat and wrote in my notebook, sipped my coffee and listened to the hum around me: the hum of many tourists who hoped they would come back to Paris. I never spoke English to the waiter, lest he mistake me for one of them.

76

Since the French were forced to be vacation lemmings in August, everyone who went away at the same time came back to Paris at the same time. The traffic was so bad that radio and TV stations announced a color code that signified how awful the tie-ups were (green was normal; orange, not great; red, awful; black, the very worst). Newspapers printed maps of France with the highways in various colors according to the worst flow. The nightly news always showed footage of the four-hundred-kilometer *bouchon* (bottleneck) that accompanied the major travel days. The bumper-to-bumper traffic seemed to be part of the ritual. Obviously there were ways to avoid it——one could travel on another day——yet it was part of the French national experience to share this misery together.

This mass return was called *La Rentrée,* (the re-entry); it was the official start of not only the back-to-school season and the wearing of fall clothes, but the fall social season. It was time to make whoopee in Paris. People you said *"bon été"* (good summer) to in July——whom you hadn't seen or heard from since——were again your best friends. The greeting was "Did you pass a good summer?"

Phones rang; e-messages flew. The mail was thick with invitations to parties, gallery openings, benefits, premieres and assorted charitable and cultural events. "What I did on my summer vacation" was a suitable topic of conversation for about two weeks. Then the true swirl of the season became a tornado . . . and soon the leaves changed and the rain came and suddenly it was Christmas.

Not only was this my first full *rentrée* in Paris, but I had a beau. In fact, I was in heat and madly in lust with the Count of Monte Cristo . . . which in turn reflected on my love for Paris. Paris was more beautiful than ever. My husband was always with me, but now he had given me permission to go on with my life and I began to find joy in every day.

I would say I was madly in love, but even then I knew the affair with the count wouldn't last, that it was infatuation, not real love. Still, I was giddy with glee. I was all but doodling his name and mine inside heart shapes in my notebooks. I began to diet.

The count was in Paris a lot to escort me to many of the season's events. To the French, Geneva and Brussels are merely suburbs of Paris. People commute quickly and regularly.

We went to the reopening after renovations party of the Hotel Meurice; opening night of Alain Ducasse's newest restaurant, a big-time movie premiere—complete with *tapis rouge* (red carpet). There was a musicale at Versailles; a bash at Galeries Lafayette where you walked through layers of red plastic streamers and ate on tables strewn with dark red rose petals. Rose petals were so "in" that any day I half expected it to rain roses.

We went to one dinner party at the Pavillon Gabriel, a private venue for meetings and dinners located across the street from the U.S. Embassy, right off the Champs Elysées. At the entry were six-foot-tall Plexiglas vases filled with sparkling water in which green apples wrapped in cellophane floated and bobbed. At the tables, white orchids were hung from wires that made them seem to float in the air. The earthbound centerpieces on each table were built from cabbages.

While I was invited to a number of events on my own or as a journalist, most of the really good invites came through the count. To have such a boyfriend was as good as seven-minute frosting on chocolate cake.

One of the events I went to solo was a party for Tim and Nina Zagat, who had launched their famous restaurant guide in a Paris edition, published in both French and English. I kiss-kissed chefs and friends from all over the world, including my friend Peter Greenberg, one of America's leading travel writers (and correspondent for *Today*) and one of my oldest friends. Greenberg—who lives in L.A. but is on the road 75 percent of the time—had not yet heard about Mike's death, so we went to dinner and had one of those old-friends-philosophical-life-is-what-it-is discussions about everything—being alone, being secure in your own skin, being able to be happy within yourself and being dropped in the middle of nowhere and able to cope and then make friends. By dessert, I had told him about the count.

"I have a quasi-boyfriend," I told him, with too much delight.

"Quasi?"

"That means he's married."

Peter's face froze. Despite the fact that we were seated in one of the fanciest restaurants in Paris where whispering was the rule, he shouted, "Kalter! What the hell are you doing? Are you nuts!"

He had reverted to my maiden name, by which I was known until my son was born.

I was shocked at his shock. I'm not sure if it was from having lived in France, or having read too many trashy novels or being blind to reality—but I wanted him to be happy for me, not embarrassed or judgmental. I felt that for my first sexual adventure in widowhood, a man who was not actually available was far safer; I thought I'd been smart about it. I thought only the American Congress was prudish when it came to adultery.

77

As I partied my way through Paris and hobnobbed with an international cross section of people, I began to see certain characteristics that fascinated me. The count, for example, despite his age, was what I came to call one of the new French—he understood marketing, he worked hard and long hours and he liked foreigners, especially Americans. He traveled a great deal and was open to the world around him. Despite the fact that by the laws of French society, especially from his epoch, he could have traded on his title and his family connections, the Count of Monte Cristo was a modern man who claimed he was most influenced by his English nanny and American GIs after World War II.

The expats also had certain characteristics that were probably not shared by our countrymen back home in the United States. To make it in a foreign country we not only needed the right stuff, but a certain kind of flexibility that fell into a category that Peter Greenberg and I had discussed on that night when we talked over all our personal philosophies. It was the Parachute to Mars theory: we believed that there is a certain group of people who flourish anywhere, whatever the challenge. If you dropped us on any planet, we would not only survive, but make friends and hate to leave.

Along with this went the ability to see the United States from a global point of view—its good parts and not-so-good parts. Many expats were embarrassed by the big deal made over past presidential high jinks and the state of limbo caused by the need to recount votes; others were embarrassed by more recent policies at the highest level. You didn't have to dump on the United States to be part of the team, but a realization that nothing is perfect was part of the general subtext. A common theme in many dinner party conversations was the number of problems in the U.S. political, school and social systems—especially health care and the cost of medicines.

While I did meet a few Americans who were unhappy living in Paris, most were blissful. Many had jumped ship and left their employers when a tour of duty was up. All loved the United States and appreciated being American citizens but they also loved being in France. The ones who loved France the most were usually aging Baby Boomers who looked into their futures in the United States, didn't like what they saw and decided to stay in France where downsizing was a way of life, not a sin.

78

My friend Steven came to Paris during the *rentrée*. Steven is the most beautiful man I know: gorgeous to look at, smart, funny, chic, with-it. He knows everyone (they all went to school together, of course) and most important, Steven is a genius from whom creative notions pour forth like the water at Versailles. He is the one for whom the bells tolled. His ideas emerge from his mouth in perfect packaging, ready to be put on the shelves and turned into money.

Whenever Steven came to Paris, we always went someplace exciting, usually the latest "in" place where only he could get the reservation. Invariably Steven wore black leather pants and a custom-made black leather shirt undone to the waist. His wrists would be wrapped in black leather and silver bangles, offerings from Hermès and Gucci and the gods. His black hair was slicked back and his tan vibrated. Were his eyelids tattooed? Everyone stared. Everyone was jealous.

Our *rentrée* date was for a Sunday night. Sunday night dinner in Paris has never been easy. Aside from the hotels, not too many places are open. As a result, there's a handful of restaurants where everyone eats. One of them is Balzar (49 rue des Écoles, 5e), which was once a famous café on the Left Bank, known as the hangout of many celebrated types. I've been there several times and have never been impressed; never even seen a celebrity—dead or alive. Word was that since it had been sold several years before it hasn't been the same. Nonetheless it was still open for dinner on Sunday and still had a full house and a full reputation.

Going out with Steven was always fun because he never failed to appreciate it if you dressed up and looked great, if you brought some theater to his theatrical being. I spent some time during the day trying to decide what to wear.

Hmm, should it be the Yohji wool wrap knit skirt with flocked see-through blouse from Berlin and a rope of tribal African beads? Maybe the tweed skirt with Aunt Helen's hand-knit vintage sweater from the '40s? Of course there was always the new plum-colored silk suit with the pink plastic Chanel booties . . .

I decided I was getting carried away. We were talking about Sunday dinner at a dumb bistro in the middle of nowhere on the

Left Bank. Why look like an overdressed idiot with a need for attention? I wore a simple black Armani pantsuit with a black crewneck cashmere sweater and black suede flats. It was Sunday and I didn't want to play the game.

Then I walked in the door of Balzar and saw the designer Tom Ford at the best table. He looked up at me, gave me a quick appraisal and then dismissed me—all in seconds. The dismissal was final. Heartbreaking. I thought I would die. If I had worn one of my other outfits, Mr. Ford would indeed have given me two seconds more. I could have been a contender. Or maybe a muse.

79

The count invited me to Italy for a few days. He went to business meetings during the day (as I recall, he was then plotting to buy the Italian phone company or something like that) and I worked on *Born to Shop Italy*. I noticed that the hotel luggage tags on my bags now said Monte Cristo, which made me grin. The doorman nodded to me and said, *"Bon giorno, Contessa."* Maybe he thought that increased the size of the tip, as it's my guess that the count had been there with any number of non-contessa contessas. Nonetheless, it was fun.

I inspected a new hotel that was so exciting I called the count on his portable phone (one of three) and asked if he was free to come meet me there and have a drink. He was delighted, he had an hour, his driver was waiting and he'd meet me in ten minutes.

We walked around the hotel and had a drink in its fabulous lobby. The count purred sexual endearments. "I could take you right here in the lobby," he whispered. Hmm, not something the average Westport housewife heard during her twenty-five years of marriage. I loved it. The count liked to talk dirty. This fascinated me as I had no experience in this arena. My husband's idea of talking dirty would be to explain a baseball play in which the runner had a nasty slide into the base.

We sat over drinks in this luxury hotel lobby while the count told me all these titillating things he planned to do to me. I imagined it would be a hot time in the old suite that night.

He went to another meeting; I went to La Perla to buy underwear and endured the prices (cost of one brassiere and pair of panties: $150) and insults about my bosom ("You mean that size *fits* you?").

I had been with the count long enough to learn some of the rules of Viagra, which included not drinking too much and taking the pill an hour and a half before you expected to need it. When you went to dinner at nine-thirty, it seemed to me you had to plan very carefully. So I was surprised and confused to watch the count consume most of a bottle of wine at dinner. Then he insisted on three after-dinner drinks in the hotel's swanky lounge. As far as I could tell, by midnight he still hadn't popped any pills.

He obviously wasn't planning on sex that night.

So what was all that in the hotel lobby earlier in the day? Why had I been to La Perla? Was it something I said? Was I no longer attractive? What was going on?

The sexual questions were confusing. I didn't understand. It made me feel shy and stupid to have all these questions, but I simply had very little experience. I felt like a nun set free at a carnival who gazes into the mirrors at the funny house, where nothing is what it seems.

I had been somewhat embarrassed about the sexuality the count had brought out in me, but I was enjoying it too. I had forgotten the power of a new relationship, especially the part that is all heat and no common sense. I bought fancy underwear— not just at La Perla but everywhere, including the Italian dime store. I took long baths again. I wore high heels again. I turned into a teenage girl and I loved it, although it was also frightening. I thought about sex all the time. I certainly seemed a lot more interested in sex than the count did. How was I supposed to be playing hard-to-get when he couldn't even play get-to-hard?

80

To escape the situation with the count, and to be a little less available and eager, I went to the United States on a quickie trip in honor of my late husband's birthday. My son thought we should go to Westport, so he drove down from Boston and I took the train up from New York. We went to the site where Mike's ashes were scattered; Aaron sang some of his new songs. Then we did a lot of errands. As we finished the ones on my list, I asked Aaron to pull into the pound, which was down the street from the house we had owned and was where we had adopted most of our cats.

"Mahhhhm," said Aaron. "What are you thinking? This cannot be a good idea."

"Look Aaron," I explained, "we just went into the Goodwill

Store. They didn't have what I needed and we left. I just need to look."

The truth was more abstract. I had wanted a dog since I arrived in Paris, but I knew it was a bad idea. I travel a lot, I had never had a dog of my own (Mike and I were cat people) and I thought it was an emotional crutch, that I needed to grieve alone and not transfer feelings to a dog. Paris was filled with women and their dogs; some were pretty pathetic partners. I didn't want to be Widow Woman with Dog Child, a grown woman who babbled in baby talk sounds in French or English to a fluff-ball animal of distinguished pedigree. On the other hand, I was lonely. And I did have my bad days, when depression was hard to beat back.

My friend Laurent summed it up perfectly. "It's better to talk to a dog than the walls."

During some of my lowest moments in Paris, I had already tried to adopt a dog. I did not yet know that once a year (in December) Brigitte Bardot sponsored a big animal adoption campaign and that it was easy to pick and choose and adopt. I certainly hadn't heard of the Fondation Assistance aux Animaux, which sponsors adoptions. Everyplace I asked in Paris had been discouraging in a very snotty way—you must raise the puppy, you must have a full-bred animal, you cannot go to the SPA (French for the pound) because their dogs are bad, etcetera. The pet stores on the quai de la Messagerie were puppy mills that I knew were dangerous.

I sort of wanted a Jack Russell, a dog that was very trendy in Paris and attracted my attention because they were being used in Chanel ads. They cost one thousand dollars, more than I could afford. When I asked for information, I was told these dogs were too high-strung for my lifestyle. The vet in my building knew only of a French poodle who needed adopting. *Merci, non.* A poodle? Puhleeze.

I was told to avoid the French SPA because they are under-funded. The dog you could end up with may have problems. A funny little mutt would be just fine, but not a totally insane one.

So we walked into the pound in Westport, Connecticut, and went directly to the dog section. Aaron walked to the end, I stopped at the first cage, my feet paralyzed on the bare cement. She was sitting there, looking at me with big, runny, brown eyes—rheumy eyes just like my Grandma Jessie. She cocked her head to one side and she smiled at me. A dog smile. According to the card on the cage, her name was Sam, or Samantha. She was the ugliest dog you have ever seen, but I was mesmer-ized by her. Her owner had died (I could identify); she was seven years old.

She was the right size for Paris, although she looked de-formed. I asked the caretaker if she was normal; he explained that her legs were the right size, but that she was so fat it was hard to tell what she looked like. She had not been groomed in years but stood there, one mess of black shaggy fur supported by four little six-inch legs with a gray beard and those eyes. She stared right into my soul. Her owner had died. Now she was on death row. I burst into tears. I knew I'd grow to love that ugly little dog in no time at all.

"*Tu parle Français?*" I whispered into her tangled, floppy ear.

Because she was more than five years old, she was half price. Since we couldn't change her name—she answered to Sam—we named her Samantha Joe Cocker. I knew so little about dogs that when the man at the pound told me she was a cocker spaniel, I be-lieved him. Although Sam is some type of spaniel, she certainly isn't a cocker—but we wanted her to be a rock-and-roll dog, so we kept the Joe Cocker part. French people always ask me what *race* (breed) she is; I just say spaniel.

Sam moved from the pound to Paris with style and a wag. She walked into her kennel at Kennedy Airport and never looked back. I think she was already conjugating French verbs or looking for the House of Madame Etre. She hit the sidewalks of Paris with élan. Her first social experience in Paris was lunch at The Gallery in the George V, where she was served water in a silver bowl and then chicken breast on French porcelain. When she went to the Hotel de Crillon later in the week, they gave her a dog tag that said IF I AM LOST, RETURN ME TO THE HOTEL DE CRIL-LON. Unfortunately, they wouldn't give me one to wear.

Sam liked Paris. What's not to like? Especially from a canine perspective. Dogs rule Paris. The French seem to like dogs more than they like children. Dogs are accepted everywhere except stores that sell food, but they do visit street markets that sell food. They are welcome in most fancy restaurants except the Ritz, Les Ambassadeurs at the Crillon and Alain Ducasse. Ducasse provides a dog-sitter.

It took a few days to get a routine worked out since whenever we went for *le promenade*, Sam refused to do her dog business because she was too busy looking for the Eiffel Tower. She also wanted to send postcards to her friends back at the pound.

She enjoyed cafés and leftover croissant bits crumbled under tables. She sniffed cigarette butts and hovered for a long time over the Gauloise brand. Empty—or semiempty—candy wrappers were especially fascinating if chocolate was involved. After a few weeks, I learned why she was so short: she drank coffee from my mug if I left it on the floor or in a place she could reach it. If it had sugar, cream or a spicy flavor, Sam wanted it. If it was dog food, she said *non, merci*.

Sam liked the freedom and the perks of being a French dog—she was taken everywhere in taxis, limos, buses and metros. Buses required that she be placed into a *sac*, so she gave new meaning to the words *doggy bag*. I bought a tote at Monoprix, rejecting the one from Louis Vuitton. She wagged her tail and gave loving licks to all she met, but licked only my feet. She'd found freedom in middle age. She might be short and fat with a gray beard, but she had inner beauty and a good sense of timing.

The best chefs in town soon knew her and cooked for her. Strangers stopped on the street to talk to her; she picked up French quickly. Because Sam was adopted, she had no history, no past. I was free to invent her. She was reincarnated as my dog princess, "the girl" and Samma-Lamma. Karen Fawcett nicknamed her Samela Pamela. I called her the royal dogness and Samantha Dog-Dog. I was worse than a new grandmother.

I became what I had dreaded. I cooked for Sam. I talked to Sam. I made up dog songs for Sam. I enjoyed her company, her personality, the fact that she had energy and soul but didn't talk too much. She liked to eat. She liked to shop. She liked to sit in bed and watch TV. Suddenly, I had another companion; one who was much easier to understand than the Count of Monte Cristo and who gave love without a hidden agenda.

I merrily entered the world of the dog, where I learned whom to call to come to the apartment for the dog's *toilettage* (her grooming, which included a spritz of dog perfume at the conclusion), what size raincoat she wore (46, just like me) and where to get a custom-made dog leash (Groyard).

Sam's personality began to emerge. She had bad eyesight which made her fearful of curbs; she stepped down gingerly. She was afraid of grates. And sometimes she just got stubborn and sat down, refusing to budge. One day during one of these sieges, I tried and tried to get her moving—without luck. A Frenchwoman passed by, looked at Sam, saw me tugging away and commented, "Hmmph, that's France for you. Now even the dogs are on strike."

There was a vet in my building, so we went to visit. She spoke English. At first the vet was confused about Sam's age, as Sam was obviously older than the seven years listed on her dog papers. But the vet thought she was a French dog and we were currently in the year of the Ts, only last year was the S year. How could I explain this?

I had no idea what the vet was talking about until her assistant realized this was an American dog and the French tradition of naming all dogs following a letter of the alphabet per year did not pertain to Sam.

81

There is a well-known French expression that translates basically into "invest in stones"—this is the same idea as Gerald O'Hara had in *Gone With the Wind* when he told his daughter, "Land, Katie Scarlett, land is the only thing worth fighting for." In both cases, it meant, when in doubt, buy real estate. It is the foundation of the French economy. It's also the basis of the concept of Yankee thrift, dating back to the Massachusetts Bay Colony. You buy real estate and you never sell.

Whether it was my fear of the stock market, influence from French culture or my desperate need to know that my son and I had a safe haven, I decided to buy a house in France. Once I made that decision, I wanted the house as quickly as possible. I transferred approximately $150,000 from the life insurance fund to my French bank account and began to fantasize that by Christmas, Aaron and I would have a new home. As the chestnuts fell to the curbs in Paris, as I walked my dog day after day in her black nylon raincoat, as I became more and more accustomed to life in France, I knew that the lack of a house was all that stood between me and my dream of feeling truly at home here.

It was time to enact the backup plan.

The backup plan was something Mike and I had created before he died. I had written it all down in the Book of the Dead, the book of notes he dictated to me during the weeks he was sick. Essentially, it was the if-everything-goes-wrong-then-what? plan that would take into account our IPO being a flop, Born to Shop dying out, my not being able to get any work, my not remarrying or anything else that would leave me up against a stone wall. The IPO was a dot com thing. It died shortly after Mike. Bye-bye, easy life. Hello, reality.

The backup plan was to buy a small house in France, pay cash for the whole thing and have very little overhead so that no matter what went wrong, at least I had a house and was safe. Things weren't particularly going wrong, but they weren't going right either. Mike's business had gone bankrupt after he died; he died at the beginning of the worst losses in Dow Jones history since 1939–1941. I was not on the Fortune 500 list of America's most wealthy women. I was a bit scared by my losses in the market, the failure of my broker to protect me and my uncertain future. I felt financially adrift. I felt a need to connect to France and to stay in Paris.

After the trip to Italy, my relationship with the count began to fall apart, which became another factor in my need to build my own life and feel secure. It was time to go house hunting.

When I told Aaron that I had decided to invest in stones and that I hoped when he came over for Christmas we'd have our own house, he was not pleased. In fact, he exploded. Then he crumbled. I would never have even mentioned it if I hadn't thought he'd be happy, have a feeling of relief that we would have a home with our own furniture from Westport and be delighted that he could bring friends over. He didn't see it that way.

"I don't see why we don't buy a house in the United States," he said, his voice breaking.

I explained that I had already looked at apartments and houses in San Antonio, that I was happier in France and besides, it was simply a good investment. French real estate had already gone up 20 percent in the time I had lived in France. I explained that I couldn't afford to live in New York or Boston. I went over the rough edges of our losses in the market. I explained the world according to me. I explained that after selling a house in the United States, downsizing only worked if you could find a great house for a lot less money. To me it was simple business and arithmetic. We were broke but could afford France.

As Aaron and I talked it over, I realized that he had not yet fully understood that I had actually moved to France. He understood that we had sold our house in Westport because there was no money for two households, but he didn't grasp that I wasn't coming back to America in the near future. Or ever.

First he lost a father to cancer; now he was losing a mother to France. My sunny bunny of a child was hurt and angry, bitter and confused. I felt guilty but also hurt. I thought I was entitled to a life and wasn't at all sure that I could make a new life for myself in the United States.

I was the one who had inherited the life insurance, the house and the problems that went with the falling market and the failure of my husband's business. I was the one who chose to put aside a hunk of money to pay for the rest of my son's education and to keep his lifestyle throughout the next years away at school as close to the way it was before tragedy. I felt stretched to my limits, but I didn't want a problem with my son. Nor did I want to move back to America just because he was having trouble adjusting to our new circumstances. I simply didn't know what was the right thing to do or whose feelings I needed to cater to—his or mine.

82

Besides, I had indeed sold the house. It was too late to reconsider staying in Westport. I chose to return to the United States to close on my house, have the tag sale of the century and put my favorite belongings into storage. I chose France.

I think that moving from your house after a death in the family is like another death. In my case, giving up the house and my personal belongings was worse than enduring my husband's funeral. I watched my husband waste away and knew when it was time for his body to die. He lives on now in my son and me, his work and our memories. But the death of a house and a lifestyle and the loss of a collection of a million bits of home history is more like being stabbed in the heart with failure and guilt. In the best of circumstances, giving up the old family home is traumatic, especially for the children. While we had lived in other houses, this house was the one that my son grew up in and it was very important to him. I knew the necessity of selling it; my son felt only the pain of departure.

For six weeks I packed clothes to be given to charities; I organized items for our tag sale; I gave things to friends and even mailed some items around the world. My girlfriend Carolyn flew up from Atlanta to help me and to haul off things she could salvage for her craft business. A friend from Paris had moved to New Jersey and came with a truck to take away enough to furnish her new apartment. Scavengers came and asked if I would give them my husband's tools or my treadle Singer sewing machine. Friends of Mike's asked for his precious sports memorabilia. Aaron showed up at the end to provide music to pack by.

I put myself on automatic pilot; and I somehow got through it all. Thankfully, I have blocked out a lot of what happened. Many of the parts that I do remember, I do not dwell on as they make for ugly nightmares. It was a difficult time made only slightly better by a few trips to the Super Stop & Shop and dreams of sitting at the table in France, entertaining my new friends. The carrot on the stick that got me through the torture of moving was the fact that I would soon be hosting an American Thanksgiving dinner in Paris.

My trips to the supermarket yielded all the fixings that were impossible to find in France. I even bought the Butterball turkey. I often packed frozen foodstuffs in my luggage in winter. The luggage hold is so cold that food will stay frozen for about twelve hours, certainly long enough to get from New York to Paris. For that year's Butterball, all I had to do was pack it and pop it into the freezer in France. *Et voilà*. I left the house with a heavy heart, and heavier suitcases.

83

When I got to the Delta check-in at JFK Airport, the woman asked me how many pieces of luggage I had.

"Seventeen," I said.

"You can't have more than nine," she announced with authority. She was quite firm on this, with an edge of nasty in her voice. I smiled and whipped out a credit card.

"I'll pay the overweight freight," I assured her.

"That's not the point," she explained. "Our computer program can only account for nine pieces. You cannot take more than nine pieces."

And then the miracle began. First, the skies parted and one of Delta's famed Red-Jackets appeared over the woman's shoulder and he spake unto her saying: "Put it in twice, as two nines."

And his name was Dalber Grim and the sun shone and birds sang and angels smiled and there was wonderment throughout the check-in area. He was living proof of the kindness of strangers; that airlines sometimes do know the meaning of customer service. He took over at the computer. With a flourish on the keyboard, all seventeen bags were checked. After I shook his hand (you don't tip management), I headed away toward the duty-free stores.

"Wait! You have too much carry-on," he said, and called me back with a wave of his hand and red-jacketed cuff. "Two of the carry-ons have to be checked, Mrs. Gershman."

Oh no, say it's not so! That would cost me another two hundred dollars, making a total of nineteen pieces of checked luggage. The charges were already around one thousand dollars. Oh *merde*.

In my dumbed-down state of anxiety I had forgotten to ask if I got mileage points, but at least one piece of my brain wasn't totally numb. I recalculated. Nineteen pieces over? Couldn't I think of anything clever?

"No!" I shrieked. "Wait!"

Everything at Delta stopped. Everyone at all of the Delta counters stared at me. Two guards put their hands to their holsters.

"One of those suitcases just has the Butterball turkey in it, for Thanksgiving," I said. "You can't charge me for the turkey; they don't have Butterball turkeys in France! It's un-American of you. It should be charges for eighteen pieces, please."

"Turkey flies free!" Mr. Grim announced and everyone applauded.

84

As soon as I got back to Paris, I put the Butterball in the freezer and unpacked all that luggage into mounds that resembled some sort of organizational system to me, but surely looked like clutter to anyone else. One suitcase had been packed in the United States and remained by the door, ready. The count had invited me to meet him in London, so in a matter of hours, I was on my way to the train station.

The count's secretary came to my house in Paris with my train tickets (first-class Eurostar). His driver took me to the Gare du

Nord and personally placed me, and my luggage, on the train. The count called me on my cell phone when I was on the train to make sure I was on schedule. He gave me the cell phone number of the chauffeur who would pick me up in London, then he warned me that he had not been given his usual room at the Mandarin Oriental and apologized in advance for the view. He preferred the view of the park.

"Oh no," I explained, "you have the good view—I bet we can see one of my favorite stores, Harvey Nicks!"

I stayed for two days, wrapped in the amenities of a great hotel and my passion for the count. It was sort-of R&R after the ordeal of the house closing. I went to my traditional London resources, took all the Jo Malone bathroom goodies from the hotel and spent hours at Hatchards buying more books in English. I loaded up on magazines at Selfridges and settled into linen sheets.

On my first night around seven P.M., while the count was in the tub, he directed me to answer the ringing doorbell. It was room service with a plate of canapés and a bottle of champagne in a large, silver bucket. I was really impressed. What a way to live! What a romantic guy! What a caring man! Was this great, or what?

We had a picnic in the bathroom and I thanked him for the treat, for helping me to recover from the ordeals in the United States.

"It's nothing," he explained. "The manager always sends a comp bottle of champagne, I just told them to hold it until tonight."

Gee, the only honest Frenchman in the world, and I wish he'd lied. It cheapened the experience to be told the picnic was a freebie, to realize that the count thought he was clever to have arranged it all. Something inside me snapped. I lost my love-is-blind attitude toward the count in a matter of less than one minute. The count went to Geneva after Day Two; I stayed with a girlfriend for an extra day to try to sort out my feelings. First-class train tickets can be changed on a moment's notice.

85

One of the reasons I chose my place Pereire apartment in Paris was that it had three chimneys—one in each of the main rooms. I have since discovered that there was even one in the kitchen, but when Herr Strumpf bought this apartment and renovated it, he pulled out the original kitchen and all its charming elements.

The broker who showed me the apartment told me the remaining chimneys did not work; I had no reason to doubt this. After all, working or not, they were a nice addition to any room. Aaron had wanted a bedroom with a fireplace in it in Boston, so I thought he would be pleased to at least have one in Paris. Working or not, the fireplaces were the swing vote in why I chose to rent the apartment.

By fall, I learned that while it was technically against the law to have a fire in the fireplace in Paris, this was a law that was generally disregarded. Most fireplaces did work; friends were certain that all I needed was a little *ramonage,* the art of the French chimney sweep. You couldn't just light a fire to check on the draft, though. Your apartment was not covered by its insurance policy if you had an accident caused by a fire unless you have had the proper chimney sweep and he has not only done the job (without singing any songs from *Mary Poppins*), but given you a certificate that your insurance company will honor.

Furthermore, there was another old saying in France that it was always your job to know what the law was even if it was hard to find out what the law was: *nul n'est censé ignorer la loi.* Pity the person who has not learned about *ramonage*.

Finding a trustworthy *ramoneur* was not as easy as you might think; this is indeed an art and since it's unlikely that you are going to climb up on top of the roof of a building that is more than one hundred years old and probably covered in clay tiles, you need someone who can be trusted up there. Although there are brochures shoved under your door and signs posted on house gates, anyone you talk to will warn you about using these free-lance guys. So you ask around to find someone trusted and then you book the appointment. Needless to say, such a rendezvous wasn't easy to get because this work was seasonal and a process that must by law be repeated every year.

You heard all kinds of horror stories about people who have not used a *ramoneur* or had not used a good one; the worst were stories about fires that jumped into other apartments because of the way the draft ran up the building. The biggest problems were caused by deposits of soot and carbon resins or by wet and humid wood from years gone by.

I used the *Washington Post* rule of three hard checks from *All the President's Men* and waited until a specific name or brand was suggested to me by three different sources. So it was with the Perduzzi Brothers, who informed me that they couldn't get to me until November. I was very keen to have the fires roaring and sad to have to wait. But it was the *rentrée,* and the time flew up the flue.

On November 4 the *ramoneur* and his assistant arrived as promised at eight A.M. M. Perduzzi was very cute, about fifty years old with curly, black hair and smily, crinkly big black eyes that had already assessed my ass; he liked to flirt, that much was clear. He treated his assistant like, uh, dirt—in the medieval fashion—but he treated me in the traditional chauvinistic manner of European men. While he sent the assistant to the roof, he walked around my kitchen inspecting everything and making small talk. Large kitchen, not often you see one this big. Was I American, English? The usual. I offered one of my magic cups of instant coffee from Italy and he scoffed at it; no—he wanted me to make him freshly brewed coffee. I explained that I only had American coffee that was *parfumé* (flavored) with nuts. He shrugged why not. I made the coffee and served it, he then ordered me around the kitchen fetching what he wanted to jazz up his coffee: brown sugar not white, milk not cream. He inspected the china service to see which pattern he liked best. He wanted a cloth napkin.

After a sociable half hour, with the assistant doing God knows what, M. Perduzzi inspected each of my fireplaces by bending into them and blowing. I never saw him lift a finger to clean anything (certainly not even his coffee cup). He charged me $150 and asked if I knew how to light a fire.

"*Bien sûr!*" I said indignantly. "*J'étais une Scout.*

His opinion of women, even Scouts (pronounced scoots in French), was chauvinistic. He motioned for me to come to the front salon fireplace. He twisted the *Herald Tribune* into a long wand and lit it with a match. Then he crouched almost inside the fireplace itself and lifted up the burning torch into the small passageway that is my flue. He was squatting there with one arm raised, somewhat in the fashion of the Statue of Liberty.

"This is the cup of coffee you must give your fireplace every time you want a fire," he explained.

"This warms the walls and gets the draft ready to pull. No coffee, not have good day in fireplace."

86

Since I no longer had a home in the United States I figured I might as well begin the paperwork that would make me a U.S. resident living abroad, a legal condition that involves a tax break and assorted adjustments to the filing system. Even though I would then have to pay French tax as well as U.S. tax, I decided to apply for a *carte de séjour*.

I knew I was in for a long and possibly frustrating experience, but it had to be done. I got the list of documents I needed and took a taxi to the appropriate ministry. The woman behind the desk did not speak English, but my French turned out to be fine. She was warm and friendly and asked to see my passport. After thumbing through it carefully, she asked where my D visa was.

"What's that?"

I truly had no idea. I had never heard of it before; to my knowledge you no longer needed a visa to visit France.

"It's the permit that allows you to stay in France for more than three consecutive months."

"But I'm never anywhere three consecutive months. I'm a travel writer. If I'm not out of town, I'm not doing my job."

"If that is the case, madame, then you don't need a *carte de séjour*. You do not qualify to be a French resident. You are a visitor."

Welcome, Shriners.

People who function in a foreign language are used to the fact that some days the adopted language flows from the tongue with ease and speed and even majesty; other days the lips turn to peanut butter and all skills stink. My visit to the ministry had impressed me; my French was more than adequate that day. I didn't think this was terribly odd; my French had gotten better in the last few month, but was still spotty. I seemed to be my most fluent when discussing philosophy with taxi drivers and my most stupid when discussing business with someone important. I was a lox when it came to eavesdropping on the count's conversations in French.

Still, an amazing thing happened that winter. I turned on the news at eight P.M., as always (*comme d'hab,* as the French say). It took me a few days to realize that I actually had understood the news in French.

I simply turned on the TV, watched the news and weather and then a *policier* and went to sleep. I took it for granted that I understood until I realized—in a flashback—what a huge step this was for me. There was a time in my life in France when I had to call the news desk at the *International Herald Tribune* to ask them to clarify a point of the news that I hadn't grasped from French TV or newsprint.

While I still wasn't fluent, or always smooth, I was now able to watch TV and to understand what was going on. Learning to speak French in middle age was one of the most difficult things I had ever done.

I was nervous about the lack of a *carte de séjour* and wanted to make sure I was indeed living legally in France. Karen Fawcett gave me the name of her accountant, an American man in Paris who worked with the expat community. Richard Van Ham was tall and handsome, with a fancy office a mere ten minutes from my apartment. Proximity in Paris is a big plus in making—and keeping—friends and relationships.

I showed him the things that I kept in the financial dossier first used when I arrived in Paris and a list of my jobs for the current year, a pathetic little list. I explained that my husband had died, I had moved to Paris and wasn't yet working full-time. I assured him that I did not work in France, which—as I understood it—was all the French government really cared about.

He asked me a series of questions, such as how many days had I spent in the United States during the year (forty-five) and did I own, rent or maintain a residence in the United States after selling my house in Westport (no). He explained that as a U.S. resident living abroad, I was allowed to visit the United States only thirty days a year, but since I had no U.S. residence, a case could be made for French residency, which would then qualify me for a hefty tax break.

"Here's what you have to do to be French," he said. He neither laughed at this remark nor seemed to find it odd in any way. He simply scribbled a short list on a memo card:

• Transfer all U.S. bills to Paris address;

- Get supplementary French health insurance;
- Buy a house in France as soon as possible. Don't keep putting it off.

He handed me the memo, shook hands, winked at me and said, "Now you are almost French."

89

Mike and Aaron and I had done Normandy together, about fifteen years ago. We had wonderful stories from Deauville that I still remember, all these years later. That winter, I did the same area with my father and his wife, who came to visit and to check out my new life. They stayed in Paris with me for a few days, then we rented a car and headed north.

I call them Sy & Y; Y stands for Yvette. I thought it was pretty funny to have a family member with a real French name (and her own saint's day), but was also glad she wasn't young enough to be named Jennifer, Amber or Heather.

Mostly we drove around Normandy. I drove, a sign that my father is indeed getting old as he used to love to drive. It's also a sign that I read French and he did not. Sy & Y were aware of the mission I had been given—they knew the accountant wanted me to buy a house and they knew the rules of the backup plan. My father went along with it all rather politely (for him), pointing out that he thought I was nuts to buy a house. I should get an apartment if I insisted on this nonsense. Better yet, I should come back to the United States, buy a house in San Antonio. He said it had to do with the repair and maintenance of roofs of houses that were more than one hundred years old. He mentioned that Normandy had specific weather-related problems that could cause added expense in the upkeep of a home: rain, floods, storms, etcetera.

My father was not a pain in the ass about his viewpoint; he made his case, but he didn't act out too much. He had some very good points. I also had one million French francs ($150,000) sizzling in my French bank account and a burning need to get my belongings out of storage and be French. An apartment looking over the sea had a certain appeal. If I bought an apartment, I would avoid many of the maintenance pitfalls of home ownership and still have plenty of benefits.

It's not easy to explain to French people (or any sophisticated travelers) why you want to live in Normandy, even though there are some very chic communities there. Most people just snarl "rain" and frown at you. Normandy has English weather; so yes, it rains. Deauville, the Norman version of Cannes, is thought to be snotty and very Parisian—almost like the Hamptons, where you see the same people in the summer that you just escaped from in the city. It's cliquey and horsey and old money or French garmento—oriented and a very closed society. While there is a large Jewish community, gossips say they are Sephardic and *not our kind*. I had in mind someplace like Honfleur: arty, commercial and with enough tourists and foreigners hanging around that I would fit right in. Maybe I would open a shop, Ma Chère Suzy. It would be open between my trips abroad. I would sell my version of The Cute. We drove directly to Honfleur.

I hated Honfleur. Really, seriously, violently hated it. Waaaaaay too touristy for me, even out of season. I couldn't find true charm anywhere. I got depressed. We drove here and there around the coast and looked at the pictures in windows of real estate agencies. I wanted to at least see a few houses and get a feel for what my possibilities were. I didn't think I could afford Deauville and therefore never looked there, but concentrated on Trouville, the St. Paul to Deauville's Minneapolis.

I also had a cutting from a newspaper that listed houses being sold person to person and included an enormous old house in one of my favorite villages (Beuvron-en-Auge), but it was a huge house with all the problems my father pointed out (and then some) and it was not near the beach. Beuvron-en-Auge is a perfect little town with only two blocks' worth of main street. Each home and shop is half-timbered. I liked the fantasy: an apple town in the middle of Calvados. The name of my first business was Apple Tree Productions, named after my family pictogram on an eggcup my mother made. A person might think it was meant to be.

But it didn't seem too practical for a widow whose command of French wasn't that good. And my father did make a lot of sense when he talked about the price of electricity and fuel. All three of us smelled the dream, absorbed the Cute, had crepes for lunch and left. It was cold and damp; it was November in Normandy. It was not romantic.

Through a real estate agent in Deauville, we found a look-see in Trouville: a small house, a fisherman's house as they call it, located a block from the sea. It had three flights of stairs, one hundred square meters of living space, no parking and sat directly on the high street. That was the good news. The bad news? The house was at the low-rent end of the high street. The curb appeal was nonexistent. Sure, I could fix up the house, even paint it blue and make it look somewhat charming and seafaring. But the whole block was depressed. There was no way this house could be made more valuable unless the entire block was gentrified. We moved on.

I found a part of the coast that I liked (Houlgate), but there was little to look at. I liked the idea of the big apartment houses right on the beach, but there were no apartments availabile. I had fantasies of how happy Aaron and his friends would be in this little town. There was a tiny synagogue a block away from the beach called Cedars de Lebanon. The local café was called Café Suzy. Maybe this was a sign. And maybe not.

My friend Laurent from Deauville told me that the villages around Deauville were fine for when you were young, but when you got old, you needed to live in Deauville. Hmm, what was he implying here?

Certainly the area seemed cute. All of the real estate brokers had pictures of adorable little half-timbered houses (with roses running up the sides) at the price that I wanted, but none was available. I wondered how to say bait and switch in French.

In short, it wasn't going to be easy—there wasn't a lot on the market, houses were pretty expensive, especially in beach communities, the cute stuff was isolated in strange locations and went to insiders who were there to pounce. Houses were sold in a day. I had actually thought my price range would command an excellent selection, that I would easily find a house and at least be in escrow by the time Aaron arrived after Christmas. I was wrong. I was not on my way to becoming French before year's end.

90

A lot of friends from New York came to visit Paris in December. Airlines and hotels had good prices; insiders knew it was a great time of year. Winters were usually milder in France than in many parts of the United States and the gala atmosphere of Christmas was seductive. My friend Dorie came to Paris too, although she comes to Paris almost every month for work. Dorie is a new friend whom I met since I moved to Paris, but she quickly became one of the stars of my solar system.

On a December Sunday, we went to the flea market at Vanves, one of our regular Sunday rituals. Sam trotted between us. On the turn in the bend, where the lower-priced vendors sell from blankets on the street, we spied a man with heaps and heaps of dishes, service for twenty-four he announced with pride. He demonstrated that all the serving pieces were there as he pointed to the gravy boat, the covered vegetable dishes, the coffeepot, the cream and sugar set. He could have had a job opening refrigerator doors on TV if they still did that kind of thing.

I was besotted with those dishes. They were so ugly they were charming: museum quality examples of art from the late sixties or early seventies—swirls of lavender, yellow and green flowers outlined in black with an olive green border. The guy was asking seventy-five dollars for the works. Did I understand him properly? He wrote it down: $75.

I looked at Dorie woefully. I did not need these dishes. I did not have any place to store these dishes. I rarely had twenty-four over for dinner. Or even lunch.

"Mike made me sign a contract that I wouldn't buy any more dishes."

She looked at me with her big, black eyes for a beat, blinked and then said, "Suzy, Mike is dead."

We both thought it over for a quick second, burst into giggles and sighed.

I bought the dishes.

91

So there I was, minding my own business, visions of sugar plums dancing in my head while I stood alone in the shower, washing my private parts. Don't ask me how, but suddenly I felt a lump or a bump or a change in the physical terrain, best described as a raised surface about the size of a dime. I calmly rinsed off, dried off and grabbed my makeup mirror then stood upside down in my petite *salle de bains,* trying to get into a decent viewing position. I briefly thanked God that I had LASIK and didn't need reading glasses, which would have fallen off, since I was forced into a variety of upside-down positions.

I'll spare you the graphic details, but there was no question that something was there and it was not a mosquito bite, or even a deer tick. It looked like a melanoma to me. But wait, no need to panic after all. I did further explorations and discovered two more lesions; I revised my medical opinion. Phew. Goodbye to melanoma. Must be genital warts, except I don't know what those are, what they look like or how a widow who was with a man who used a condom on the rare occasions he could get it up could have a sexually transmitted disease.

I went online to learn more. I read medical papers in French. What's a little language difficulty at a time like this? In only two days of translating I decided that I probably had cervical cancer. I called my brother in Texas, an oncologist, and arranged to go to San Antonio to see a specialist. I asked Yvette to get me an appointment with her OB-GYN in San Antonio for a second opinion. I bugged Claire ten times a day, wondering if I was going to die, if I should be treated in France or go to MD Anderson, the famous cancer hospital in Houston. Should I tell Aaron?

Claire suggested that instead of making both of us crazy, I should go see her doctor and then have the U.S. doctor as a second opinion. Is Claire a genius, or what? She called the man who has been her doctor for twenty-five years and who delivered both of her children; he agreed to see me immediately as an emergency case. I spent the taxi ride to his office wondering how to say *tata* in French. The office was in the sixteenth, in a fancy building with fancy offices where I waited in what looked like a salon of the Hotel de Crillon. The doctor came to fetch me. He was middle-aged and balding with cute little half glasses and an Hermès tie: he was perfect for the part.

I filled in no forms; was not asked for insurance cards or Blue Cross Blue Shield preadmission codes. The doctor took a medical history by hand on stationery with a fountain pen. We began in French, but I was forced to ask him to speak more slowly, explaining that I didn't speak French very well.

"I can speak in English then," he said. "I was trained in America."

After my explanation of the problem, he stood up, gestured

to another room with an open palm and said, "Prepare yourself." Then he left the room.

Prepare myself for what?

There were no gowns of either linen or paper; I wondered briefly if I could convince the folks at Porthault to go into this as a line extension. I got naked and waited for the doctor to return. When he did, I stared at the elaborate crown molding. It occurred to me that crown molding was invented by a woman in the exact same predicament who didn't know where to look or how to focus her attention.

In short order *le médecin* told me that I had neither a melanoma nor genital warts nor even herpes, but some harmless lession that could be taken care of in a blink. I explained I was getting a second opinion in Texas, which did not seem to offend him. He asked if I wanted to have the removal and biopsy done in Texas or when I returned to France by him. I had trusted him the minute I met him and now knew immediately that he was my guy. I felt suddenly very French and asked him to do the surgery. If I chose to live in France, then French medical care was also my choice.

The doctor in Texas was also wonderful; he confirmed that I had nothing to fear but fear itself, that of course a biopsy must be done, but no biggie here. He did, however, think I needed a D and C because of the constant bleeding I had at a time when I should no longer have a period. I wondered how to say D and C in French.

The two doctors together handled all the paperwork and my French doctor sent me to the clinic on a specified day. Clinic to me meant clinic, like maybe an animal clinic for people. I faintly recalled that Madeline went to the clinic to have her appendix out. When I got to the clinic, I almost burst out laughing. It was not an animal hospital, but an eighteenth-century mansion set behind wrought-iron gates up a curvy driveway sequestered in the middle of the sixteenth. This was a private hospital of the first rank. The lobby and check-in area looked like a hotel's; the herringbone wood floors were polished to a glow; the staircase would make a bride happy; the waiting rooms were painted high-gloss white and furnished with white leather sofas. The women all looked like Catherine Deneuve. They were dressed in suits, stockings, high heels and carried designer handbags and fancy overnight bags. Some trailed furs. All had recently been to the hairdresser. There were few men waiting there.

There were problems with my admission since I did not have French health insurance. But how will you pay, asked the nurse at admissions. I told her that I would write a check. Her eyes grew wide, she gasped, for the whole amount? Obviously, this was not the common practice and this was going to be expensive. I didn't tell her that the fees would be paid from my late husband's life insurance policy.

Pascale-Agnès came into town with her husband and moved into my apartment in case I needed help. She called on my mobile to announce that there was a hair dryer in my *salle de bains,* did I have another hair dryer to bring to the hospital or should she bring this one to me? I said I did not plan to wash my hair while in the hospital, *merci.* There was a silence, then P-A said, "It's not for the hair on your head. It's to dry your pussy."

P-A and Thierry came to the hospital bringing all the things I didn't know I needed: the hair dryer, a pillow, a robe, some comforts of home. For a nightgown she chose the dress I had washed by hand and left hanging in the bathroom to dry. It was dry now, but was also a three-hundred-dollar Donna Karan slip dress, not a nightgown.

I had a private room with private bath and TV, but there were no pillows for snuggling, just the standard hospital bed that goes up and down. For reasons that remain unknown to me, there was a Darth Vader quilt on the hospital bed. Thierry left us to our woman things in the woman hospital, as any French husband would do. P-A stayed with me for several hours until they took me away for the surgery. I don't remember too much more. The anesthesiologist made jokes and was funny; he obviously gave me good drugs. The last thing I remember saying to him was, "Will I have pain, doctor, or will it be bread?"

I thought that was very clever at the time and actually don't think it's too bad now.

After I left the hospital, I recalled only that the bill for everything, including the blood work, lab work, private room, drugs, doctor fees and biopsies was just under one thousand dollars. Why can't America have a health system like this one?

92

It's a well-known fact that stress leads to illness. In closing up the house in America, I'd suffered a terrible cold. I knew it was a stress cold. While I rarely got the flu, I decided I should get a flu shot. I was convinced of this while passing my local pharmacy, where the workers are very patient with my French, are always kind to my dog and help me a great deal with medications. There was a sign in the window that said something like YES, YOU CAN GET YOUR WINTER FLU SHOTS HERE.

I thought, *great, what a civilized way to do this—I'll just pop into the pharmacy and have a jab.* I walked in, ordered the flu shot and rolled up my sleeve, figuring they wouldn't have me pull down my knickers right there in the shop. The pharmacist came back to the desk and handed me a small cardboard box. *Voilà.*

In France, you got the medication for the shot at the pharmacy and either gave the injection to yourself, were given the injection by a family member or made an appointment at a clinic to get the shot (doctors do not give shots). Rich people had a nurse come to their home to shoot up. I went to the vet downstairs in my apartment building.

93

Perhaps the first time I truly understood the meaning of ritual was after I became a mother and began to create or sculpt events to give my son a sense of balance. I am big on rituals of the Jewish faith, rituals of the commercial holidays, rituals of return and renewal; traditions of home and family. Of course, you never know what your children will take with them in their basket of memories, but we mothers stand ready to stock the picnic basket then stand back and wait.

With a death in the family, I turned again to ritual. I had a funeral for Mike so that Aaron would have its memory to give him peace. I found comfort in old rituals or the creation of new ones. Rituals give you roots; they even provide a way of coping. Rituals have structure to them and when you don't know what else to do, you can always fall back on what has always been done.

In my first year in France, with Mike's death behind us and a whole new way of life in front of us, Aaron and I were on our way to creating new rituals: a language between us to help us grieve, to mark time and to bring stability. Tradition is invaluable; leaving traditions behind is what makes parting so sad. With the holidays approaching, and then the anniversary of Mike's death, I thought we were headed into some emotional days and much pain.

Aaron wanted his Thanksgiving dinner as he had celebrated in the past few years, with his friends from high school in Westport. He wanted Christmas and New Year's with them as well. Then he announced he and his band would come to Paris to be with me for the anniversary of Mike's death, which I had taken to calling Dead Day. We decided to make up our own rituals to mark the date.

My son, the very young man who for several years refused to go to the ocean with his father and me to throw rice into the sea on New Year's Day, told me that he was ready to observe this family custom. We agreed that when he arrived in Paris, we would throw rice in the Seine from the Bateau Mouche . . . for the new year and in memory of our beloved.

94

When Thanksgiving arrived in Paris, I cooked my fifteen-pound Butterball in Mike's mother's turkey roaster, as I had for the previous twenty-five years. My French friend Richard called to wish me happy Thanksgiving.

"Are you cooking the donkey?" he asked.

At first I just thought this was a giggle of a gaffe. Richard was flustered.

"*Excusez-moi,*" he begged, "I got the word turkey mixed up

with the French, *dinde,* and the second half of turkey and it came
out wrong."

The Tuttle family came to dinner, as did some of Les Girls. It
was fun, I wasn't depressed at all. I made all the usual foods
from our traditional feast, many of which had been brought over
from the Super Stop & Shop in Westport, Connecticut. I had
brought cornbread stuffing mix, pumpkin pie mix, canned sweet
potatoes and a huge bag of marshmallows. I was only missing the
buttermilk biscuits . . . impossible to re-create since they don't
have buttermilk in France.

Food at a time like this is about tradition, or perhaps all traditions are also about food. Food is comfort; having enough
food is being thankful for life insurance. Of all the daily in-
sults in widowhood, I did not find my first Thanksgiving in
Paris to be difficult. It was a celebration of life and new friends
and the chance to bring them some new traditions from my
neighborhood.

Other widows have told me that of all the holidays, Thanksgiving was particularly hard for them. Others have confessed
that all sit-down meals, especially family meals, are hard because
the husband's place is obviously empty. It never crossed my
mind to be upset or confused. I set the other head of the table
for Mike and we left it empty. I felt that it was a bit like the rid-
erless horse in the regimental funeral, the turned stirrups showing a fallen warrior.

My family never had a Christmas tree; my mother said we were Jewish and didn't have Christmas trees. When I married Mike, he said yes, he too was Jewish, but that not only did his family have a tree, but Christmas was important to him. He really *wanted* a tree. We agreed to celebrate Christmas and Channukah. More chances to shop; yippee.

So I decided that I needed a Christmas tree that first year in Paris. I also decided that I would buy it on Thanksgiving weekend. There were several reasons for this, one of which was my desire to have the tree buying and decorating as part of the Thanksgiving celebrations. Mike always made me wait until December 15 to buy the tree. Without him, I could do whatever I wanted. I also wanted the tree in place early because of a December date with the count, whom I was still seeing occasionally even though the initial sparks were gone.

I tried to interest him in the notion of going out for the tree and decorating it together as part of our celebration, but he said he never did that with his family and he certainly wouldn't do it with me. Ouch. Things with him were going steadily downhill; any attempts to set it right seemed doomed. Still, we had planned our own Christmas together on an arbitrary date in December since he would have to be with his family in Évian for the real holidays.

I bought him many gifts, which I wanted to be waiting for him under the tree. I also bought new Christmas stockings, as it seemed tacky to use my family stockings with another man . . . and one who was married to someone else.

The French aren't that big on Christmas trees—especially the older generation. Christmas trees, as we all remember, came into fashion in Victorian times when Prince Albert brought the custom from his native Germany. The English and the Americans took to the idea, making it a more and more elaborate tradition as Christmas became more and more commercial. The French never gave up as much of the religious overtones of Christmas as other cultures and tended to do seasonal house decorations, that may or may not have included a small tree. Big, bold trees with heaps of ornaments and even a theme to their décor are a relatively recent idea—brought along by retailers who have had success selling Halloween in France and figure anything is worth a try. Hotels and artists jumped into the enthusiasm by getting together to create exhibitions of unusual or artistic trees that up until that point were always in the realm of the French florist.

It's also possible that big, fat, fabulous Christmas trees haven't caught on in France because the trees here are, well, ugly. If you think that everything that grows in France is divine, you are right—except when it comes to pine trees.

Christmas trees in France, which are ranched, come in two varieties (*épicéa* and *normandie*) and neither is perfectly formed. The Norman tree can cost two or three times as much as the plain old pine, but the pine sheds its needles. While the tree may have some density at the bottom, invariably by the time you get to the middle and above, there are enormous spaces between the branches. This calls for a very clever eye to decorate the tree and to fill in the blanks (so to speak).

Our family ornaments had gone into storage with the rest of

the things I was keeping when I closed up the house; I kept just a few crystal ornaments that Mike and I had bought on our honeymoon and our Christmas stockings, but I needed to start anew. I bought ornaments from Galeries Lafayette. As it happened, that particular season Jean-Charles de Castelbajac, one of the enfants terribles of French creative style, had designed a group of colored ornamental balls, each with a different verb representing the twelve desires of Christmas. I thus learned the verb *oser* (to dare) from my Christmas tree.

Since it was my first holiday tree in my new homeland, I was anxious to deck the halls . . . and the branches. I used three ropes of lights, which in France are doubled, so the lights were tightly packed to fill in the thin branches. The Castelbajac ornaments were each in a different pastel, metallic color with the verb printed in bright gold letters. I spaced beaded fruits on other branches—not tacky, kitschy beaded fruits, but the kind that were meant to look sugared. They were very Old World and rich in hues, dusted to perfection in shimmering beads. To my eye, each looked like a Judith Leiber evening bag. I had apples in three different colors, pears with streaks of rose to red across their fat bellies, lemons and aubergine plums—surely they were sugarplums. On top there was an old world angel with a banner that read GLORIA. My mother's name was Gloria. My tree was decked in French and Latin words: the roots of my new life.

96

Like every American child, I knew how to pronounce the French word *oui* from an early age, knew that it was usually used as a double, as in *oui oui* . . . and most importantly knew, tee hee, that wee-wee was urine.

As I began to speak French, some thirty years later, I pronounced *oui* as "wee," as I thought was appropriate.

No longer. Now I live in France. My accountant says I am almost French.

I say "way" like everyone else.

97

Before Christmas, the count and I spent four days in Cannes, including one perfect Sunday when we went to Grasse to visit some friends of mine at their villa. The trip was pretty rocky as I kept confronting the count with the problems with the relationship and the things he needed to do to change. He kept avoiding confrontations, then began avoiding me.

Our sex life had pretty much gone to hell; he no longer even kissed me goodnight. I knew that it was just a matter of time before I left him, not just because of the sex but because of the almost constant strain that I felt when I was with him. I was always trying to please him and he seemed never pleased, or was unable to acknowledge that he was pleased and that my efforts were worthwhile. I knew that I needed to be out of this relationship. It wasn't a question of "he loves me; he loves me not," I decided, it was merely "do I leave now or after Christmas?"

Then suddenly that Sunday in Cannes, it was decided for me. My count decided to tell me some of his sexual fantasies.

So maybe I'm a prude. But I was disgusted.

I just had to figure out what to say.

98

Back in Paris, I hired a limo to take us around Paris to look at the holiday lights and then drop us off at the George V where a small, private dinner party was being given by some of my friends to celebrate the end of my first year in Paris and to introduce the count to our group. These plans had been made well in advance of our trip to Cannes and my realization that there were things about the count that I could not tolerate. It was all pretty bad timing, but a date was a date . . . and I was still trying to figure out what to say to him and how to leave him as gracefully as possible.

I ordered champagne for the car; we snuggled into the back seat under a mohair throw. It might have been romantic. Instead, the count pulled out his cell phone and began to wheel and deal. As he talked in many different languages, I would occasionally nudge him and point at the holiday decorations. At first, he'd look and nod but after a while, he waved me off, as if to say *leave me alone.*

I couldn't decide if I should sulk or not. You treat your wife that way, not your mistress, I said to myself—me, the great expert on mistressdom. In between a group of calls, the count tapped on the glass to get the driver's attention and asked him to head over to the Four Seasons Hotel George V. The tour was only half done. I had planned it all, checked on the best decorations and coordinated the route with the limo driver. I was hurt . . . and pissed off.

"Seen one set of lights you've seen them all," he shrugged and began punching buttons on his phone again.

I stepped out of the car close to tears and not at all in love. I told the driver to charge the toll to the count's account, not mine—a small act of revenge and childishness that made me feel instantly better. I told myself this man would not ruin my evening and that I was not defined by how he treated me.

He was charming at the dinner and I was quite proud of him. This confused me even more. Was he a nice guy with a few sexual problems, who happened to be very busy . . . or was he a creep? I pushed to the back of my brain the problems we had been having and the debilitating doubts about the future of this relationship, but after the dinner, one of my friends pulled me aside to help me with my coat.

"Look Suze, you're a grown-up and I know you're lonely after Mike's death, but you do know that this man is not our kind, don't you?"

We broke up that night. I went back to the Meurice with him, packed my things and simply told him that adultery didn't work for me, that I needed more from a relationship. His lips pursed together in a flat line, he stood up, buttoned his jacket stiffly and walked to the door, which he opened for me. Sam trotted out behind me.

She was smiling.

We got into a taxi and went home to the seventeenth. I sobbed all the way home. Sam sat in my lap and tried to lick the tears on my face.

99

The Tuttles were being so nice to me it was almost disgusting; everyone was oozing empathy, because the holidays and the anniversary of Mike's death were approaching and also they knew I had just broken up with the count. They wanted me to feel loved, they wanted to help me through this triangle (Christmas, New Year's and Dead Day) and they were genuinely worried about me, although I am sure I didn't seem to be suicidal, since I wasn't.

Instead, I felt as if we were all part of some farce or vaudeville, a countdown to Mike's *yahrzeit* (anniversary), and we all just needed me to get there and then get past it, to finish up the dreaded first year and get on with life.

On Christmas Eve, I took an overnight tote and went to the Tuttles', to have a sleepover date. We had a family dinner and a movie out and then I went to sleep rather early. I just wanted to escape and get through it all. Christmas Day started off well enough with presents for all and a very quiet family time of padding around in our pajamas and drinking eggnog and eating waffles. We got dressed around noon and other guests began to arrive around one P.M. These guests were the Tuttle Christmas regulars, who had this holiday and this territory staked out long before I arrived in France. I found myself drinking eggnog and trying to be amiable in French with a group of people I had just met but who had known each other for years.

Among the guests was a sixty-year-old divorced dentist. This was not a fix-up, Claire made clear. He was a regular on Christmas and one of their best friends. For the most part, he ignored me, but as we drank more and more eggnog (Claire's specialty; it does not come from a carton in France and is made with crème fraîche) he chatted with me a little bit and we somehow got into a conversation about women.

"Believe me," he said with a Gallic curl of the lip, "I know everything there is to know about women and what they want because I am a Frenchman."

No, I wanted to say, *you are an asshole.*

But I didn't say it. Instead, I steamed. I smiled outside and I fumed inside. I looked around the room and outside of myself and wondered what the hell I was doing here.

You're here because your husband is dead, my brain said back to me, the word *dead* echoing throughout my being. *Dead, dead, dead.*

You're here because now you live in France and you left home, home, home, home. These people are being nice, nice, nice, nice. You gave up America for this.

The enormity of the whole year stood up in the Tuttles' fireplace and laughed at me. I was a stranger in a strange land making small talk with a chauvinistic pig and it made me sick. In fact, I went into the bathroom and threw up. Then I gathered together my things, went into the kitchen and told Claire that I wasn't doing so well and walked out the door, without saying goodbye to the others. I went home to Pereire and went to bed. Sam and I had a dog nap.

I was fine a few hours later, but resolved to do the rest of the season my own way.

100

There was no lack of invitations for New Year's: pity invites, I called them. Thanks, but no thanks. Christmas had been too upsetting. I preferred my own company. Or Sam's company. Aaron was arriving shortly and with his visit would come the celebration of the anniversary of Mike's passing. I really didn't want anything else dramatic or traumatic. Mike and I were never big New Year's Eve people anyway.

The widow division of Les Girls was doing New Year's Eve at Myriam's apartment overlooking the Eiffel Tower, then they were driving to Provence on New Year's Day. I couldn't go to Provence with them because of Aaron's arrival. I knew from previous New Years that it was virtually impossible to get a taxi in Paris on New Year's Eve, especially after midnight, and I didn't want to spend the night. There also seemed something sad about girls' night out, and while I really loved their company, it was too painful to contemplate spending this New Year's with them. Three Widows and a Dog: it sounded like a bad Woody Allen movie. I felt no need to be doing something just to be doing something.

I simply wanted to be home alone . . . with Sam and with Mike, with some boiled little potatoes, French *demi-sel* butter and a jar of fresh caviar.

Since I wasn't going to join them in the evening, we widow girls decided to meet for lunch at The Gallery at the Four Seasons Hotel George V, one of our regular hangouts. Sam also liked it there, in fact, she was so well known that she was allowed to wander without her leash. Normally Sam went from table to table, she was petted and fed a few tidbits. She had the drill down pat. For some reason, that December 31, of all days, Sam changed her routine.

She simply fell in love with a middle-aged man seated a few tables away and would not leave his feet. I glanced over at her a few times—we all noted a look of total contentment on her face as she sat at his expensive shoes, panting. The man looked European, mid-sixties, rich and, as the French say, *sympa*. Actually, he looked something like Mike. He just seemed like a nice guy. Sam seemed to think so too; she was giving him the big brown-eyed doggy stare.

When it was time to leave, I kissed Les Girls goodbye, wished them Happy New Year and went to retrieve my dog from the thrall of this total stranger. We began to chat. He was Italian, from Milano and spoke only French and Italian, but somehow he understood my French and I understood most of what he said. He asked me to join him for a coffee. We talked for two hours. When I finally said I had to go, he caught up my hand in his.

He said he was traveling alone, just to enjoy Paris. He apologized for making the suggestion at the last minute, but he wanted to dare himself to ask if by any chance was I free this night, and if so, would I like to have dinner with him.

I saw no reason to be coy. Or to be alone when such a seemingly nice man was also alone. I agreed and gave him my card.

My dog found me a date for New Year's Eve.

He called me at home a few hours later to explain that he could not get dinner reservations anywhere in Paris because of the fete, but that his hotel had space in the dining room. *Hmm*, I thought to myself.

At nine P.M. a car arrived for me and whisked me off to The

Ritz. I then realized that he had said he was staying at The Ritz but I had misunderstood . . . I thought he said he was from Biarritz. Suddenly it was New Year's Eve in the formal dining room of The Ritz.

We had a lovely dinner and at slightly after midnight I said I had to go home. We walked to the front of the hotel where the car was waiting.

"I feel like Cinderella; it's time to leave the ball," I told him. "Now I go home to the ashes."

"No," he said, "you will always be my princess of The Ritz."

And I stepped into the waiting car, laughing.

The flowers arrived the next morning.

And a new year began.

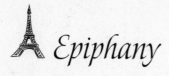 *Epiphany*

Café Les Hortensias, place Pereire, 17e
Pour boire: espresso

I don't know why it took me so long to discover Les Hortensias, a café on another corner near the front door to my apartment. Although only a few steps from the Royal Pereire, my headquarters during my first months in Paris, it was a whole world away—so chic, so upmarket, with yellow walls and dark green trim. The chairs were dark red, woven wicker shining bistro chairs, new but in the old style and designed with heart and chosen by someone with taste. It was a pleasure to sit there and be part of the parade.

I didn't really like espresso. I took it like medicine as it was cold and dark and I had so much to do that week. Epiphany was January 6, but the whole first week in January was a slow time in France. People didn't kick back into the work mode until after Epiphany. Epiphany also came to represent the anniversary of Mike's death, which technically was January 4, but fell into the Twilight Zone of the first week of January when everyone was waiting for the new year to start.

It was a time of reflection, New Year's resolutions, preparations for my son's arrival and for the big party I was giving for him and his friends. It was a time that stood alone for its odd subtext in France and in my own life.

For hundreds of years it has been French tradition to show off a new home with a party nicknamed the *crémaillière,* from the expression *pendre la crémaillière,* meaning to hang the saucepan on the hook over the fire. Of course, when the tradition started, there were only fires to cook on, so when the saucepan was hung the house was ready. Nowadays, instead of an open house (which is called an open door in French and does exist as a social event), French people invited all their friends for the *crémaillière,* given as soon as the new home is set up and functioning—usually at a point just under one year after arrival.

I never gave myself a *crémaillière* when I moved into the Paris apartment, but I decided that I would have an open door on the Sunday of Epiphany as a way for my French friends to meet Aaron and vice versa. Also, Aaron was coming with the members of the band he was part of at that time, so there would be music.

It was almost a year since I had arrived in Paris, so it was also a way of launching the apartment—although most of the invitees had already been to the apartment for dinner parties. I scheduled the party from three to seven P.M. so that I could serve desserts. Then I made an even more radical decision. I decided that it was time that I cook French. Goodbye Betty Crocker. *Bonjour tarte tatin.*

When I first came to Paris, I did not have the gall (excuse the expression) to cook French. In my first year, I even based my reputation on serving American food at my table. But as I began the preparations for the open door, I knew I was almost French.

My welcome-to-France gift from Patricia Wells had been what she called the best *tarte tatin* pan in the world. I had yet to make a *tarte tatin* because I was so intimidated by the idea of cooking French, but I had the pan. Inspired by my friendship with Dorie Greenspan, one of America's foremost cooking experts and a woman who specialized in desserts, I decided to get out of the frying pan and into the oven. I told myself to test a few recipes. Dorie told me I could do this. Of course, she was writing a cookbook and thought everyone could do it, but I wanted to believe her.

I made the first *tarte tatin* as sort of a trial for myself. When I finally did it, it was easy and tasted fabulous. I grinned inside and out; now I am truly French. Lafayette, I have arrived. Should I call the accountant? Did I still need to buy a house to be French when I could master a *tarte tatin*?

Having successfully climbed this mountain, I was bored.

My next *tarte tatin* was influenced by my grandmother's ruggeleh and my Texas upbringing. I soaked yellow (muscat) raisins in cinnamon *sirop*, then mixed the raisins, along with bits of pecans, into the apple mixture for the *tarte tatin*. It was stunning. I began to wonder why you didn't see more variations of *tarte tatin* in different bakeries or restaurants, so I asked around. I learned the most basic of French rules: if you changed the recipe, then it wouldn't be a *tarte tatin*. (In France, it's always about the rules, dummy.)

So it was time to move up the next rung. I decided to try a *clafoutis*. Heretofore I had not been a big fan of this custardlike dessert from the south, but Dorie had made a terrific one and converted me outright. She was testing the recipes for her book *Paris Sweets* and baked all day, tasted and then gave away the desserts. Dorie was still a size 4; I was almost a size 16.

Dorie's cherry *clafoutis* was beyond sensational; I would get up in the middle of the night to pee and then wander into the kitchen to have a slice of *clafoutis*. I wept when it was gone; I went into *clafoutis* withdrawal. The only reason I didn't ask for the recipe or sign up for private *clafoutis* lessons was that I knew I would never fit into my clothes again. But I was hooked and knew I needed *clafoutis* for my party.

I bought a book on *clafoutis* (*Les Clafoutis de Christophe* by Christophe Felder, the pastry chef at the Crillon and the French king of *clafoutis,* editions Minerva, about $25, in French only). The only thing that held me back from testing each recipe in the book was my bottom line; that's right, the size of my bottom. Besides, not all of the *clafoutis* in the book were desserts—some were more quichelike.

While doing the grocery shopping for the party at the big Auchan hypermarket in La Defence, I discovered the Alsa brand of *clafoutis* mix. (Which I have since found in the grocery store of my local Monoprix.) Could a girl resist? I bought a jar of pitted cherries marinated in red wine. To the chagrin of my chef and foodie friends, I have always been the sort who will use a mix rather than bake from scratch. At least I always admit it.

When the testing began a few days before the party, there were immediate stumbling blocks on my way to *clafoutis* triumph, such as the fact that I did not own a one-liter liquid measure. In my effort to convert from milliliters, I poured two beakers of 500 milliliters into the mixture, then realized I was supposed to have added 750 milliliters. *Okay,* I said to myself, *pas de problem.* The box came with two sachets, so I added one half the powder from sachet number two. Furthermore, I was using a thirty-centimeter *tarte* pan and the recipe called for twenty-four centimeters, so I had a little extra room. (*Phew!*)

But the mixture was very runny and I panicked. A finished *clafoutis* is a solid creature. This was a milk bath that could never get it together, as far as I was concerned. Who to call? Alain Ducasse? One of my GM friends who had come up as a chef like Richard Duvauchelle? Perhaps Patricia Wells? No, only the Queen of Clafoutis would do.

I called Dorie at seven-thirty A.M. I knew the Clafoutis Crisis Center would be open. But people like Dorie Greenspan do not cook from a mix; she knew little about my newest problem in life. We agreed it would be folly to add more powder; that I should bake the sucker and see what happened. Dorie kept saying the viscosity should be somewhat like a quiche. Here we were, back to quiche.

So the *clafoutis* went into the oven and I went into my office. I forgot all about a timer or the time and did not even remember that I was baking until twenty minutes past when the clafoutis in a twenty-four-centimeter dish would have been ready. Yet when I opened the oven (bake at number 7 in French oven), the *clafoutis* was gorgeous—with patches of golden brown that danced across the top. The only problem? It was still total liquid. And to make matters worse, my doorbell was ringing.

It was the telephone repairman, making a miracle visit right after the holidays.

"Where's the damaged telephone line?" he asked me.

"Quick!" I screamed, "to the kitchen!"

I showed him my *clafoutis*; I explained it was my first one and I was worried about all the liquid.

Oh no, he said, it was a fine *clafoutis*; it looked great.

"It will congeal when it cools, or you can put it in the fridge to congeal it more quickly."

Only in France would the telephone repairman know how to rescue a *clafoutis*.

103

As my life in Paris began to stabilize and I felt fewer and fewer reasons to treat myself to something special in my husband's name, I gave up my weekly visits to the floral market for fresh flowers. When I first moved to Paris, I gave myself many small luxuries in Mike's name—things to help me through the crunch of the first year of widowhood. Mike bought me fresh flowers every week when he was alive, so I saw no reason for him to stop just because he was dead. But with the first year over, and my budget becoming more real, I decided it was time to stop splurging. Fresh flowers were no longer needed.

As I prepared for the party, however, I faced a daunting hostess problem. One of the guests was Jeff Leatham, creative director of the Four Seasons hotels in Europe, the man who did the flowers for the George V hotel, the Four Seasons flagship in Europe. His creations there were so extravagant that he had become famous; he was featured in magazines all over the world. Tourists went to the hotel just to stare at the flowers. As a hostess, I wanted something dramatic and stunning on my mantel, so I wouldn't embarrass Jeff—or myself.

It would have been easy enough to go back to the flower shops and toss around lots of money and come away with baskets of fab flowers. But I didn't want to invest in something that would die after a few days. I was past wasting money. I decided to explore the option of fake flowers.

I should have known that when it came to style, even fake style, no one can beat the French. With a little research, I discovered two options—a handful of designers who were famous for their fakes . . . and the wholesale silk flower district. Emilio Robbia had wonderful arrangements, but they were just that— formal arrangements. I wanted single blossoms. So I went to Harvé Gambs's shop on the Left Bank and bought an armful of faux amaryllis. Then I went to the flower district in Paris for more silk flowers. I filled in a few stems from the Sia boutique . . . and some from my discount shops and street markets.

Loaded with a wide range of elaborate silk stems, I made one of my California-style arrangements—an homage to the days when we lived in L.A. and I made floral combinations in a riot of color and texture.

When my mantel was completed with the new arrangement, I stood back and smiled. I felt delighted with the visual impact of the presentation, but shared a moment's philosophical joy with myself as well. It was a small triumph, but a real one. I had spent more than a thousand dollars during the past year, and many hours, messing around with just the right fresh flowers. It had been incredibly important to me, as a tribute to my late husband, as a ritual to perform on Sundays and as a way of telling myself that I lived in Paris, where beauty was around every corner. Suddenly I discovered that I was more secure, I didn't miss this ritual. Indeed, it was almost a metaphor for my whole year in Paris—I had arrived with one notion of what was right for me only to discover another way to get an equal, or better, result.

104

Aaron and his band arrived about noon on January 4, the actual anniversary of Mike's death. We had planned to all go on the Bateau Mouche, the boat that circled Paris, to throw rose petals in Mike's memory—instead of our usual rice—into the Seine. I bought silk rose petals, thinking they would float. But the boys had jet lag when they arrived and wanted to sleep.

Two days passed; Aaron showed no signs of being ready to do the tribute to Mike. I wasn't going to push it. I had thirty people coming for Epiphany. I baked. I tested more recipes. I went out to buy *fèves* (the charms that went into the traditional French three kings cake, called a *galette*) and paper crowns for all those who would get *fèves* in their portions. The celebrations for Epiphany were geared toward children, but everyone got involved—a phenomenon that interested me as a marketing device created in the Middle Ages.

Since medieval times it was accepted knowledge that holidays made the time pass more smoothly and gave people something to look forward to. Holidays broke up the grind of everyday work; holidays were a payoff for a lifestyle that was cruel and without other relief. Epiphany was twelfth night, the day on which Christmas gifts had originally been exchanged. Modern times had switched gift giving to December 25 and left the days in January an utter bore. To make it worse, the French didn't have the Super Bowl to break up the winter gloom. So they devised a series of games and treats for the Epiphany holiday, one of which involved the spinning of a cake in front of a group of people. Each person got a slice, starting with the youngest. One person found a charm in his or her cake and was therefore proclaimed king or queen. The person was crowned. Everyone was happy.

Each of the many desserts I made for the party had a *fève* inside it, even my American chocolate cake with chocolate frosting.

105

The guests were a delicious mix of American expats, French friends who did not even speak English, families with one or two generations in tow, retailers I knew from Born to Shop or my regular shopping haunts, service providers (my hairdresser), neighbors from the building (yes, even the concierge stopped by) and a few strangers, who were either brought by friends or who were in town for the last holiday of the Christmas season and who called to get in touch. It was easier to invite them to a gang bang than a one-on-one, especially when my time then was devoted to my son.

When Jeff (FlowerBoy, as *People* magazine dubbed him) Leatham arrived at the door, he held out a giant plastic bag filled with fresh rose petals. I had told him the plan for the Dead Day tribute.

"I couldn't stand you using fake flowers," he said. "Have you done it yet?"

"No," I sighed. "We're not ready yet."

We put the fresh flowers in the *frigo* and went on with our party.

As those things go, it was a good party. I wore comfort clothes and showed off my new earrings, created by a jeweler friend in Providence from Mike's and my wedding rings. The boys played music, the guests ate all the desserts. As I raced around the apartment, I surveyed guests from four different countries spread out in my kitchen, dining room and living room. A fire burned in the living room, under the new silk flowers. A few of the guests were wearing golden paper crowns. Many of them were people I didn't know a year before. Now they represented my French family.

Life handed me a lemon when my husband became sick and died. Somehow I had made *citron pressé* . . . and it was sweet.

106

Paris in January is not the downer that January can be in other parts of the world. The weather is relatively mild, there are parties and activities and even the sales to look forward to. The week with the boys passed amazingly quickly; it was fun to have the house filled with people and filled with music. No word was ever mentioned about Mike's anniversary service. There were no tears, no scenes of whimpering or breast beating. The day before he was to leave Paris, Aaron asked me if the rose petals were still in the fridge.

Yes, I said, of course.

"Do you think Dad would mind if instead of doing the Bateau Mouche thing, I took the flowers to Père Lachaise and Jim?"

My husband had been friends with Jim Morrison in the music business in the late sixties and early seventies. He had gone to Miami with Jim for the rock star's obscenity trial. Of all Mike's rock and roll friends and clients, he and Jim were particularly good friends. Now Mike and Jim were dead. Mike's ashes were in Westport, Connecticut, but Jim was buried in Paris at the most famous cemetery in the world: Père Lachaise, just a metro ride away from my apartment. I think that to my son, a singer-songwriter still coming of age, Jim represented one of the things he had lost when his father died—an important and intangible connection to the music business. It seemed altogether fitting that the flowers go on Jim's grave.

After Aaron left for the cemetery, I sat alone in the apartment for a while. I thought I was moving forward and that I was ready to start the new year. But I kept thinking of the Bateau Mouche, and Mike and my wedding ring earrings. I realized that I needed my own ceremony.

I took the bus to Pont Alma, where the Bateau Mouche is moored. I headed toward the river, but before I got there, my favorite café, Chez Francis, beckoned to me.

I sat inside the glass windows and stared out at the Eiffel Tower and the passersby. I thought about Mike and his sister Judy, and all the times we had all been to this café together. I thought about how lonely and empty I would have been if I stayed in New York. I thought about the accountant and his directions to me, and the idea of the house I would soon buy.

It grew dark. I was not sad, but calm and perhaps for the first time since I arrived in Paris, truly peaceful. I felt stable. I was going to be all right.

As I left the café and looked over my shoulder for one last glimpse at the Eiffel Tower, the lights on the landmark burst on and twinkled in their flickering chorus for ten long minutes. I stood there as my eyes welled up. Mike was on my shoulder.

Then I wrapped my pashmina around my neck and headed to the bus stop. Who needed the silly Bateau Mouche? It was time to go home and cook dinner.

"C'mon Sam," I said to the dog, "*Allons-y.*"

Afterword

Many years ago, when my husband was still alive and Paris was merely a place we visited frequently, we went to dinner in an old-fashioned Left Bank bistro with Walter and Patricia Wells. They brought along an American woman named Johanne Killeen, Pat's best friend and a famous American chef with restaurants in Providence and Boston. The five of us had a delicious dinner in every sense of the word—the food was great, the wine was smooth, the conversation was brilliant. We were all more funny, more *sympa,* more connected than any other group of friends ever.

When we got into our taxi to head back to our hotel, my husband said, "That's what living in Paris is supposed to be like. Dinners like that every night."

Now that I have lived in Paris for over four years, I can say that Mike's thoughts were not a dream but a prediction—most evenings out are as magical as that one at Café Allard. I eventually had to make a point to stay home with my dog and watch TV one or two nights a week, otherwise I wouldn't be able to cope with so many good times . . . or get any work done. And I surely would have gained more than the five kilos that have found themselves tucked onto my waistline. It's not that living in Paris is just about eating and drinking, but my life here is very much about my community—the way old friends and new friends have come together to support me.

I miss my husband every day, and I still speak to him just about every day, but I found what I came to France for. My son got used to the idea and eventually came to live with me after his college graduation.

Somewhere after Year Two and into Year Three of widowhood, I felt a weight lift and I seriously settled into my new future. I will never be the same person I was when my husband was alive and I lived in the United States, but I think I am the happiest version of the new me that I could be. Moving to France was the right choice for me.

In Year Two, I spent several months looking for a house in Normandy and bid on a perfect little pink stucco cottage in Deauville. Yes, it even had a trellis of pink roses growing up the front. My first bid was rejected, so I entered three months of limbo during which I negotiated with the owner. During this time, I went to a party in Paris honoring Walter Wells and was reunited with Johanne Killeen. She expressed her condolences and asked what I was doing now that I lived in Paris, if I was going to stay. I told her I was bidding on a house in Normandy.

"Oh nooooo!" she said, "that's all wrong! Come South, come to Provence. George and I have a house there. You know Walter and Patricia have a house there. Join us, the weather's great and now is the time you should be with family."

A woman standing next to us, whom I had just met five minutes before, echoed Jo's words. "We need you in the South of France" she said. I believed her.

Six weeks later, I bought a small *maison de ville* in the same village of the northern Vaucluse as Pat and Walter. It was a rather simple little house, but it overlooked an entire city of Roman ruins; the front windows were positioned right over the Street of Merchants. I took that as a sign. Then I hired the *mason,* and *l'équipe.* I redid the house, and by the next year was able to move my furniture from a 1962 builder's colonial in Westport, Connecticut right into a three-hundred-year-old stone townhouse in the South of France.

A few months after that, at a dinner in Provence, I met a man—single, age appropriate, religion appropriate, financially appropriate. But then, that's another story . . .

Acknowledgments

This book has been an emotional potboiler without *bain-marie*, impossible to endure without the help of family and friends to whom I offer up thanks forever. My son, Aaron James, is the best kid in the world; his father would be so proud of him and he has been part of the creation of this book throughout its many forms. I thank him for helping me with *C'est la Vie,* for helping me through the journey of the last few years, and for being my baby boy. He also named this book.

My thanks also to the editing team and my dear agent, Alice, who tried to be patient with me, and who held my hand even when I was typing. Thanks go to Diane Johnson for literary therapy and emotional support and to Stephen King, who changed my life—and these pages—and taught me so much.

Merci mille fois to Pascale-Agnès Renaud, this book's French editor, who, as always, proved herself invaluable in my move to France, and to Jacques Borene, who did the final French spell check and added his own two centimes' worth to these pages. *Ma chère* Dorie and my rock Claire get my thanks and love for being there for me; ditto to all of Les Girls: KVF, SSC, MMC, AQHW.

Please note that this is a work of nonfiction woven together to represent my first year in Paris. However, in order to give the story better flow, some of the events in this book took place in Year Two. I have also eliminated the depressing parts. You won't miss them at all.

Also note that Paris has changed enormously in the years I have lived here. Prices of appliances have gone down, Leroy Merlin (the French version of Home Depot) has come to town. It is easier than ever to live here.

Appendix 1: Real Estate Lingo

Real estate ads have their own lingo in any language; the trick in France is to not only speak French, but know the slang and the abbreviations. *Pierre* is stone, so most old buildings are described as being of stone—if it's poured concrete, the ad will say the building is new. Most stone buildings are further modified with *gd stand,* which means grand standing—a big, old-fashioned building your *maman* would be proud to have you live in.

Since an elevator was still a luxury, the ad usually announced if there was an elevator (*asc*) but rarely pointed to the lack of *ascenseur* (*sans asc*). If the apartment wasn't a total dump, it was in *bon état,* in good state, meaning in good condition. If it was a disgusting wreck, the ad usually said something like needing a little refurbishment, *au rénover* (to renovate), or *au refraiser*—to refresh, which really means to renovate as well.

The *séjour* is the living room and the *salle à manger* is the dining room, but the ads usually mention either *séjour* or *double séjour,* meaning you could use the other part of the *séjour* as a dining room . . . or an office or whatever you wanted. You could get an apartment with a SAM—*salle à manger* (full dining room)—or one with *cuisine man* (an eat-in kitchen).

Most French apartment buildings have divided bathrooms. This information was written in a number of ways—wc is water closet, where the toilet stands. *Salle de bains* is a bathroom with bathtub, unless it's noted that there's only a *douche* (shower). New apartments were attractive to the local population because the bathrooms were larger and tended to function better. Bidets were not that common; they took up too much space. You mainly found them more in hotels than in Parisian apartments.

The *cuisine* (kitchen) was either *équipée* or *non-équip,* and could be in the style of a *cuisine américaine,* which meant it was an open kitchen in a corner of the living room. *Grande cuisine* meant the kitchen was big enough to eat in.

A *balcon* (balcony) meant the windows opened onto a ledge; a *terrasse* meant the space was big enough for you to stand on comfortably and maybe place a table and chairs, a big luxury in Paris.

Because most of these buildings were old, the decorative touches counted for a lot: *plafond* or *haute de plafond* meant high ceilings. Since all rooms have ceilings, if it was mentioned at all, it usually meant they were higher than average or special in some way. The average height of the ceilings in old Parisian apartments is twelve feet; note that higher ceilings require scaffolding if you plan to paint. Really high ceilings also meant you could put in a mezzanine, or sleeping loft, which maximized space.

Cheminée is the fireplace, an excellent selling point; *moulures* is molding—another selling point, but not as big a deal as a fireplace. I looked at several apartments with fireplaces only to be told they could not be used.

Few apartments, especially old ones, have closets so if the ad said *placards,* it was unusual and considered a big plus. Why are there no closets? Because most of the apartment buildings in Paris were built between 1860 and 1890 and closets weren't invented then. (Closets are a post–World War I creation.)

Cave means there is a caged space in the basement for you to store things; *parking* means you get a parking space included; *possibilité parking* means you can rent (or buy) a parking space, usually in the building.

Most grand old buildings have been carved into zillions of tiny niches and apartments and nooks with and without crannies. I learned to go by the size of the space rather than the number of rooms. Many old apartments have odd little spaces that make for great offices; you may even read an ad that says *poss bureau* meaning you could use some of the space for an at-home office.

At the end of an ad it might say: *part.* For quite some time I thought this stood for *partager* (to share) and that the space was a time-share. It turned out it stands for *particulier,* meaning an individual, and you dealt directly with the owner. This meant you avoided paying a fee to an agency and could sometimes bargain on the price or what was thrown into the soup.

Since a lot of the apartments are co-ops, monthly rent is composed of two parts: the rent itself and the charges, which include steam heat, electricity in the hallways, the concierge fee and other extras. On average, charges are $150 to $300 per month for a two-bedroom apartment in a good neighborhood. Even if you owned the apartment outright, you still paid the monthly charges—which are an awful lot lower than the maintenance charges for New York apartments. If the sum listed in the ad was the total rent you paid, the ad said *charges comprises.*

You paid for your own electricity and water, as well as phone lines and cable TV. The amount of juice in any given building was often related to the age of the building, so many Americans preferred new buildings, which were wired for modern life and modern needs . . . or modem life and modem needs.

Appendix 2: Bedtime Stories

Because each part of the bed is so expensive, there are many cost-cutting devices and bed styles in France, including the use of slats or pallets so that a box spring doesn't even have to be purchased. For only a few hundred dollars, you can buy a trap that looks something like a medieval instrument of torture (The rack! No, no! Not the rack!) that takes a cheap mattress and lets you off the hook, so to speak. I did test one of these contraptions and swore I would never be French enough to tolerate it.

There's another style of French bed frame created specifically so that you do not have to use a box spring—it is thin, somewhat flimsy looking and doesn't look very comfy. It isn't. The mattress rests on a simple slab frame, often Japanese, oriental or French *moderne* in design and very sleek to look at.

I was doomed to want an old-fashioned kind of bed, the kind we have in America, the kind you must buy in a French department store, so I paid top dollar. I didn't know in my first months in Paris that cheapie beds are often sold in markets (try the Sunday market in the fourteenth at porte de Vanves; not the flea market but the regular food and dry goods market), over the phone or online.

Once you figure out the style and size of bed you want, you then have to think about bedding. Bed supplies cost much less in the United States than in France, but may not match up size

wise. Therefore I created Suzy's Bedtime Stories as a cheat sheet
I kept in my wallet:

- There are two sizes of single bed (90 centimeter and 120
  centimeter), two sizes of queen-sized beds (140 centimeter and 160 centimeter) and two sizes of king-sized beds
  (180 centimeter and 200 centimeter). Bedsteads come in
  these sizes also although antique bedsteads are most likely to be 120 centimeters, which is actually the same size
  as an American double bed.
- Sheets in America cost much less than sheets in France but
  may not fit a French bed. Twin sheets will fit because an
  American twin-sized bed measures 93 centimeters. And
  a French twin bed is 90 centimeters. If you buy a 120-
  centimeter bed, you can use American sheets marked full.
  American queen-sized sheets will fit on a French 140-
  centimeter queen bed, but not a 160-centimeter queen
  bed because the American queen measures 150 centimeters. A U.S. king-sized sheet can fit on a bed created by
  putting together two French twin beds. A California king
  sheet will fit the longer (200 centimeter) French mattress
  in a French king. Everything else is up for grabs.
- A French bed will fall right through a U.S. bedstead.
  Slats must come from the United States or be made to
  measure in France.
- Randy Newman, a singer-songwriter who had a hit with
  a satirical song called "Short People," has not written a
  song for tall people. When he does, he will explain that
  tall people often don't fit into French bedsteads. My son
  (six feet five inches) went through two bedsteads before
  we could fit him in.

Appendix 3: Stocking Up

The French use the expression *branché* to signify that you are with it when in fact it literally means plugged in. When I walked into my kitchen, checking everything to make sure I was ready for Aaron's arrival, I was staggered by the amount of electronic machinery I had collected in such a short period of time.

Later I learned that many Americans in Paris use American electronic products that they have set up with transformers, but I didn't know about that or how to do it and never even considered it. I figured when in France, do as the French. Use 220 voltage.

So I too was plugged in. I had two coffee makers (American coffee and French coffee); espresso machine; toaster; microwave; coffee grinder; food processor; blender; *batador* (mixer wand); washing machine; iron; refrigerator. I would have had a clothes dryer, but I was told that it wouldn't work in my apartment—I later discovered this was not true, but no longer cared. The old-fashioned system of drying clothes worked just fine for me.

The above items were in the kitchen. Scattered elsewhere were two television sets and VCRs; an answering machine; a sewing machine; three phones; two CD players; two French alarm clocks; a computer (which spoke French better than I) with jet printer; half a dozen lamps and a vacuum cleaner. This does not count the bodies of the three broken telephones I went through in the first year, nor the three answering machines.

Pascale-Agnès deemed that I was *bien équipée,* but then she checked my cleaning supplies and my *frigo* and shook her head in dismay. All French *frigos* had to stock these basics, she explained: two types of butter, sweet and salty; backup package of UHT milk for when and if I ran out of fresh milk; lardons; fresh lemon; at least one ready-made pastry roll (Herta brand is best); a selection of mustards and vinegars and a jar of cornichons; thirty-three-milliliter bottles of both flat and fizzy water; fresh eggs; and cream.

My pantry had been well stocked from my early days: one big-haul shopping event at Auchan had supplied me with toilet paper, baggies, paper towels, cling wrap and *confiture.*

From the United States, I brought Skippy peanut butter (crunchy); microwave popcorn; Ms. Dash; cream of tartar; Wick Fowler's 2-Alarm Chili Mix; nacho cheese dip in big jars; American cake and brownie mixes along with cans of frosting; foil bags of peanut butter cookie mix; Nestlé chocolate chips; maraschino cherries; maple syrup; Bisquick; and foil-sealed bags of southern pecan coffee from HayDay/Sutton Place Gourmet.

Appendix 4: A Bushel and a Peck

WEIGHT MEASUREMENTS

metric	U.S.
1 kilo	2.2 pounds
500 grams	1 pound
225 grams	8 ounces (1 cup)

BUTTER MEASUREMENTS

100 grams = 1 stick

OVEN TEMPERATURES

130°C	250°F	gas ½
140°C	275°F	gas 1
150°C	300°F	gas 2
160°C	325°F	gas 3
170°C	325°F	gas 3
180°C	350°F	gas 4
190°C	375°F	gas 5
200°C	425°F	gas 7
230°C	450°F	gas 8

Appendix 5: And a Hug Around the Neck

When my mother gave me "the speech"—the one about the birds and the bees and good girls and bad girls—she told me to beware of necking because it led to petting and petting led to sex . . . which led to pregnancy. She didn't tell me anything I didn't know. In fact, my entire reaction to the speech was the silent acknowledgment that *necking* and *petting* were the stupidest words I had ever heard. I wondered where they came from.

Enter the Count of Monte Cristo and my dog, Samantha. When the count and I were in bed, he often whispered *caresse moi,* touch me. When Sam came into my life, I learned that the verb to pet a dog was the same one—*caresser.*

Voilà! The word *petting* came from the French. Of course.